MW01273127

**PersonaCoach
Productions**

PersonaCoach
Productions

"Allan, you nailed it!"

~ Greg Clowminzer
Professional Speaker ♦ Executive Coach ♦ Leadership
Coach ♦ Business Coach ♦ Life Coach

"What an 'aha' moment!"

~ Adrienne Gardner
Personal Development Coach

"This book is very relevant to the problems that I have encountered and have seen other coaches experience as well."

~ Anthony J. Perez
Founder and CEO of Success is a Language Inc.

"I am very impressed with your program."

~ Ginette Chandler
Certified Life Coach

"I like Allan's approach!"

~ Susan R. Meyer
Owner at Susan R Meyer, Coaching & Consulting

"Thanks Allan for putting things into perspective. I could not agree more!"

~ Ulla Wiegand
Persönlichkeits-Coaching für Führungskräfte

This is such good information. Thank you Allan.
~ Veronica King
Business Improvement Specialist at Pro-actions (London South East) Ltd

Thank you for sharing this valuable information Allan!
~ Patricia LeBlanc
Certified Law of Attraction Advanced Practitioner and LIfe Coach * International Best Seller Author ***Reiki IET***

This is brilliant because it is something I have struggled with in the past. Valuable!
~ Grace Graham MSc, MInstLM
Coaching Consultant and Parent Specialist

Allan, I believe you have just helped more people than you can imagine with this information! Thank you for sharing and not keeping this valuable knowledge to yourself.
~ Kim Ravida, ACC, CPC, ELI-MP
CEO at Kim Ravida Coaching

Change Your Perception.

Change Yourself!

" Everything we experience is filtered by

our own unique perception of reality!"

~ Allan N. Mulholland

The perception of "Who You Are" is responsible for the situation you're in TODAY!

Change Your Perception.

Change Yourself!

Allan N. Mulholland

Results Coach and Perception Expert

Author of
"Clients Don't Pay for Coaching.
They Pay for RESULTS!"

ISBN-13: 978-1515342656

ISBN-10: 1515342654

This book is dedicated
to my three sons,

Justin, Daryn and Brandon

*You three are perfectly aligned
with my ideal perception of what
sons should be like!*

TABLE OF CONTENTS

Introduction

Introduction

This book will not change who you are, but it will change the *perception of who you are!*

The *perception of who you are* is the way in which others see you. It is the way in which others define and characterize you. It's what others talk about when they talk about you. And that *perception of who you are* is responsible for the situation you're in today!

• If you're not attracting the right partner to build an ideal relationship with, it's because of the *perception of who you are!*

• If you haven't landed that dream job or promotion, it's because of the *perception of who you are!*

• If you're not successful in any aspect of your personal or professional life, it's because of the *perception of who you are!*

The *perception of who you are* is your mirror image. It may resemble you in every way, but it's only your reflection.

And it's two-dimensional!

The dimension that's missing is your Identity!

Over the past 10 years, I have coached 100's of clients in the areas of relationships, career, business, addictions, health & wellness, personal development and spiritual growth. I have been privileged to help many of them achieve their dreams, goals and objectives.

I always had my own philosophy on coaching and counseling! I never accepted the limitations that traditional coaches place on themselves. I am always goal-oriented and results-driven in my personal life and when my clients hire me as their coach, they also want to achieve results!

Many life & business coaches still offer the traditional coaching methods of *"listening, empathizing, asking questions, inspiring and motivating"*.

Yet this traditional coaching model will not teach you how to make life-altering changes!

It will simply guide you on a *'path to nowhere'*.

Clearly, you deserve much more than that!

So, while my coaching methods were unorthodox and certainly not 'traditional', many of my clients achieved incredible results! But sometimes a client would relapse and go back to their old ways of doing things! And we would have to start the process all over again!

This was very frustrating to me!

Some of my clients were not achieving lasting results and I was determined to find out why they would go back to the old ways of doing things and how I could prevent this from happening by creating permanent change in anyone!

YES, I mean EVERYONE!

The answers came to me as a result of some totally unrelated events and experiences. By themselves, these events and experiences were just 'interesting conversation pieces'. But when I started to 'connect the dots', there emerged a pattern of questions and answers that ultimately led to the creation of my Signature Coaching Program: *"Change Your Perception. Change Yourself!"*

"The greatest secret to creating lasting change, is the discovery that we can alter our lives, by altering our perception"

First, let me introduce you to the villain who is ultimately responsible for the situation you are in. No, that villain is not a politician! It is not your employer! It isn't even the economy!

So can you guess who this villain is?

Probably not, because you were never properly introduced. Yet this villain has been a part of you for all your life! This villain has even tried to take over your *Identity* by pretending to be YOU.

Yet clearly, this 'villain' is not who YOU want to be identified with!

In this book, you'll discover the four stages of your *identity* and how these different stages conspired to create the *Persona* that is responsible for the situation you're in TODAY!

And unless you are successful in most major areas of your life, this *'old' Persona* has failed you! In fact, the true villain is your *old Persona* and 'IT' is responsible for all that has happened to you in the past!

• If you're unhappy with your present job - your *'old'* *Persona* is to blame!

• If you are not successful in your business - it was your *'old' Persona* that failed!

• If you created a dependency on drugs or alcohol - it was you *'old' Persona* that created this addiction!

• If you are overweight or out of shape - your *'old' Persona* is the cause!

• If you have lost your faith - it was your *'old' Persona* who abandoned it!

With *"Change Your Perception. Change Yourself!"* you will:

   i.   Change the perception of who you are.
   ii.   Create the perception you desire.
   iii.   Develop a new *Persona* for the *"person who would be successful!"*

This is the "person" *you* must become!

Imagine that you are given an opportunity to start your life all over again! To create a renaissance for the person that carries your name!

Imagine that you are given a second chance at achieving the results in any area of your life that have always eluded you!

Now imagine that you can create that second chance regardless of your age!

At the end of this book you will make some crucial decisions about the person you are destined to be, the way you want to be perceived and what you absolutely MUST achieve to give your life purpose and meaning.

Now look at a calendar and find today's date. This is where you are today! All the days, weeks, months and years prior to today's date only served one real purpose!

To get you to where you are today!

Whatever happened in your life prior to today is no longer relevant! The only significance lies in the present! This moment! This day! TODAY!

Today holds the opportunity to bring you whatever and wherever you want to be tomorrow!

But tomorrow is elusive and always conditional!

Today, you possess the equity of your actions from the Past. The residual of all the investments you have made in your lifetime. These investments may have been financial, physical, emotional, spiritual or intellectual. And whatever the sum total of these investments has produced to date, its value is determined by what you can use today or carry forward to tomorrow. These investments include your experiences, your knowledge, your health, your wealth, your family, your friends, your loved ones and your spirituality.

They all carry value, but only to the extent that they can help you achieve your goals and ambitions in the Future. This is your 'Equity of the Past' and it's the only leverage you have over your Future! Your ability to succeed at anything you do in the Future will be determined by the choices you make right now, right here.

TODAY!

"Change Your Perception. Change Yourself!" is a powerful way to become successful at anything you do, any challenge you undertake and any goal you want to achieve.

Decisions need to be made immediately about what MUST be done! No more contemplating what you should do or what you would like to do . . . someday! Today is the time to act decisively, with extreme courage and a clear vision.

No more dreaming or procrastinating. No more hoping, wishing and praying that someday you'll make all the changes necessary to make your Future more significant than your Past! From this day forward, you will leverage that precious commodity called 'time'.

So decide today what it is that you will do! WHAT YOU MUST DO!

Then make the commitment to follow through and develop the tenacity to act right away. Your window of opportunity will be closing at a rate of 24 hours per day, so you have no time to waste!

If you have one more opportunity to become successful at anything you do, what will be your absolute MUST?

• Will you try to make that connection with someone special?

• Will you go after that dream job or career?

• A new business perhaps?

• Are you finally going to lose those extra pounds once and for all?

• Are you going to re-affirm your commitment to your spouse, children and family?

• Will you quit smoking, drinking or taking drugs?

• Will you commit to getting in shape, eating healthy and living beyond one hundred years?

• Are you ready to discover the true meaning and significance of your life?

At the end of this book, who will be staring back at you in the mirror?

• Will you follow your dreams?

• Will you use this opportunity to turn a dream into a vision?

• Or is that vision just another dream?

• Is your career filling you with passion?

• Or is it just a means to pay the bills?

• Do you live and love your life without limits?

If you're not, then now is the time to create a new *Persona* for the *"person who would successful"* and for you to become that person!

IMPOSSIBLE?

Not if you're ready to commit TODAY to creating a new *Persona* for Success!

"Change Your Perception. Change Yourself!" is very powerful! It can and it will change everything about you! It will change your life and your destiny! And the best part about *"Change Your Perception. Change Yourself!"* is that you already know how to do this! In fact, you create new and different perceptions about people and things every day! Perhaps you just never realized at a cognitive level that you were applying the principles of *"Change Your Perception. Change Yourself!"* on a daily basis and therefore you never understood its amazing power, its incredible significance and the immeasurable value it brings!

The book you're about to read and the strategies I'm about to share all emanated from a single statement:

We are never who we are,

yet that's precisely who we are!

~ Allan N. Mulholland

With *"Change Your Perception. Change Yourself!"* I will attempt to unravel one of the most perplexing and paradoxical questions of human behavior. But more importantly, I will focus on the unique values and opportunities that *"Change Your Perception. Change Yourself!"* presents to all of us.

The areas in which *"Change Your Perception. Change Yourself!"* can be applied are virtually limitless.

- From weight loss to addictions.

- From the work place to the sports arena.

- From relationships to being 'suddenly single'.

- From health to wealth.

- From the spiritual realm to the corporate helm.

"Change Your Perception. Change Yourself!" can be used in every area of your life. Not only will this book show you how to play the starring role you were born and destined to perform, it will also show you how to write the script, direct the performance and stage the opportunities for success!

For once, you will feel completely in control of your life and totally confident about your outcome.

Let's raise the curtain and aim the spotlight at you!

The stage is set, so get ready to act!

Let's bring on your new *Persona*!

Allan N. Mulholland

♦ ♦ ♦ ♦ ♦

PersonaCoach Signature Coaching Program

MODULE I
Mirror of Perception

Outline

- The "Mirror of Perception" is a two-way mirror.
- When you look *into* the "Mirror of Perception", you will see your *self-perception.*
- *IF* you could look *through* the "Mirror of Perception", you would be able to see how that impression is *projected* onto others.
- If you *look back* through the "Mirror of Perception", you would be able to "see" what perception others have about you!

As I mentioned in the introduction, this program will not change your True Identity, but it will change your *perceived identity!*

Your *perceived identity* is the perception you create about yourself and project onto others. It is the way in which others relate to you. It is the way in which others define and characterize you. It's what others talk about when

1

they talk about you. And that *perceived identity* is responsible for the situation you're in today!

• If you are not attracting the right partner to build an ideal relationship with, it's because of your *perceived identity.*
• If you haven't landed that dream job or promotion, it's because of your *perceived identity.*
•If you are not successful in achieving the results you're looking for, it's because of this *perceived identity.*

Your *perceived identity* is like a mirror image.
This image may resemble you in every way, but it only creates a *perception* of you.

If you enjoy watching police stories on TV, you are undoubtedly familiar with the "interrogation room". It is a sparsely furnished and austere room where a suspect is taken after an arrest. The suspect is seated behind a table and stares into a mirror that is mounted on the wall. Sometimes the suspect walks up to the mirror and tries to see through it, but all he sees is his reflection.

The reason the suspect can't see *through* the mirror is because the interrogation room is well lit, while the "secret" room on the other side is kept in the dark. This way, the interrogators who are seated in the "dark room" have an opportunity to observe the suspect without him knowing it. How does he behave? Is he nervous? Restless? Fearful? Composed?

By looking *back through the glass*, the interrogators are able to create a *perception* about the suspect based on his behavior and mannerisms. But if the lights were turned on in the "dark room", the suspect would be able to see *through* the mirror where the interrogators are seated.

The "Mirror of Perception" is also a two-way mirror!

When you look *into* the "Mirror of Perception", you will see your *self-perception.* The image you see is the way you *currently* perceive yourself. It is the *impression* you have about yourself.

IF you could look *through* the "Mirror of Perception", you would be able to see how that impression is *projected* onto others. We all *project* an image of how we perceive ourselves onto others. We do so unconsciously. And because we are unaware of this *projection*, we pay no attention to it. Yet this *projection* of our self-perception becomes an *impression* of "WHO we are", "WHAT we are" and "WHY we are" in the eyes of those with whom we come into contact or connect with! It becomes our *perceived identity!*

IF you were able to *step behind* the "Mirror of Perception" (the "dark room") and look *back through the glass* at your *image*, you would be able to "see" the impression others have created about you. You would be able to "see" what perception others have about you.

In order for you to achieve any Desired Outcome, you must *change* these three perceptions. Specifically, you must:

1. Change the *perception* of "WHO you are", "WHAT you are" and "WHY you are". In other words, you must change your *image*

2. Change the *projection* of "WHO you are", "WHAT you are" and "WHY you are". In other words, you must change the impression you make on others!
3. Change the way in which you are *perceived* by others. In other words, you must change the impression others have created about you!

This book will show you how to change these three perceptions and as a result, *change yourself!*

♦ ♦ ♦ ♦ ♦

Signposts:

1. When you look in the mirror, do you see an image of the *"person who would be successful"* in achieving your Desired Outcome?

_____

_____

_____

_____

_____

2. Does the image you currently see represent "who you want to be"?

_____

_____

_____

_____

_____

3. When you *project* that image onto others, how might they perceive you?

_____

_____

_____

_____

_____

4. What are some of the reasons, why your image must have a "makeover"?

_____

_____

_____

_____

_____

5. Write a simple description of the "person you want to be" and explain why you want to be that person.

_____

_____

_____

_____

_____

In Module II, I will take you through the "Cycle of Identity". It is a *perpetual cycle* that can either create a powerful and purposeful new *identity* for you that will achieve the Desired Outcome you are looking for . . . . . or it will keep you on the hamster wheel that you've been treading on for most of your life!

If that's the case, then now is the time to *break that cycle!*

Change Your Perception. Change Yourself!

MODULE II
Cycle of Identity

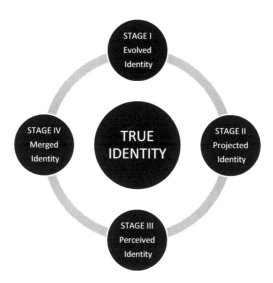

Outline

- Almost everyone suffers from some type of *identity crisis* as a result of the perpetual "Cycle of Identity".
- In STAGE I, you stand in front of the "Mirror of Perception", where you will see the image of your current *identity*. This *identity* has evolved over time.
- In STAGE II you *project* this *identity* onto everyone you connect or come into contact with!
- In STAGE III your *identity* will be defined and characterized by your INFLUENCERS. This effectively removes any *control* you have over your identity!
- In STAGE IV, the identity that was created *by* you in STAGE I, merges with the identity that is created

for you in STAGE III to produce a brand new *merged identity.* Over time, STAGE IV will "evolve" into STAGE I of the next cycle!

- Unless the "Cycle of Identity" is interrupted or broken at this point, it will continue to evolve in perpetuity!

In this Module, I will introduce you to the (r)evolving nature of your *identity* and the impact it has on the RESULTS you want to achieve. If you want to change any *outcome,* you must first change the *perception* of "who you are"! And it all starts here, with the "Cycle of identity"!

Almost every client I've ever coached, suffered from some type of *identity crisis*! And while they may not be aware of this *internal conflict,* most people truly *don't know who they are!*

If you were to ask the president of the United States if he considers himself to be a *good* president, he would likely reply in the affirmative. His *self-perception* would certainly confirm this and millions of voters would agree! To them, the *perceived identity* of the president would be positive.

But for millions of Americans who didn't vote for the president and do not agree with his policies, their *perception* of the president's *identity* would be the opposite!

So, is the president's *identity good* or *bad*?

Well, that all depends on your *perception!* If you're a democrat, you're *perception* will probably differ vastly from that of your republican neighbor!

Indeed, the *approval rating* of any president fluctuates constantly as a result of major shifts in *perception.*

While this example may be an oversimplification of the "Cycle of Identity", it illustrates the objective of this Module. Everyone you come into contact with will have a different *perception* about you. Some *perceptions* will be favorable, while others will be negative.

Cumulatively, these perceptions can be responsible for the success *or failure* you experience in any given situation.

> *The perception of "Who You Are" is responsible for the situation you're in today!*
>
> ~ Allan N. Mulholland

The good news is that you can change this *perception.* You can break the "Cycle of Identity" to achieve a different outcome by changing the *perception* people have about you.

In the political arena, parties will spend millions of dollars in propaganda (advertising) to change the perception voters have about a certain candidate. Now you to achieve the outcome you desire, by changing the *perception* you *project* onto others.

You're going to develop a new *Persona* that will allow you to achieve the RESULTS you're after!

But before you can start to develop this new *Persona*, I need to take you through the four STAGES of the "Cycle of Identity!

STAGE I – Evolved Identity

In STAGE I, you stand in front of the "Mirror of Perception", where you will see the image of your current *perceived identity*. It is important for you to understand that:

Every type of identity is a perceived identity!
~ Allan N. Mulholland

There is only one exception, and that is your *True Identity*! I will delve deeper into the meaning and significance of *True Identity* later in this module, but for now it is important for you to know that every type of *identity* that is discussed in this module (and throughout this course), is an *identity* that is based on someone's *perception,* whether that's a *self-perception*, a *projected perception* or *perceived identity.*

It's no wonder that you may suffer from an *identity crisis!* Which *identity* is *perceived* and which one is *real?*

The simple answer is that *every* identity is both *perceived* . . . . *and real!*

Perception is reality in the eye of the beholder and when left unchanged, *perception becomes reality!*

For simplicity's sake and to avoid repetition or confusion, from now on I will refer to your *perceived identity* simply as your *identity.*

OK, let's go back to the "Mirror of Perception" where you are seeing an image of "who you are". It is your *self-perception.* But this *self-perception* did not materialize overnight! It is the result of a lifetime of experiences, influences, conditioning and exploitation.

This is your *evolved identity!*

This *evolved identity* is the result of:

- **Experiences**
    - Successes
    - Failures
    - Wealth
    - Poverty
    - Trauma
    - Joy
    - Upbringing
    - Jobs
    - Education
    - Etc.
- **Influences**
    - Family
    - Friends
    - Employers
    - Mentors
    - Environmental
    - Etc.

- **Conditioning**
  - Social
  - Religious
  - Political
  - Cultural
  - Etc.
- **Exploitation**
  - On the job
  - In the community
  - In the family

Your *evolved identity* is the *starting point* from where you begin the process of developing a new *Persona*. But it is NOT the "Restore Point" from where you will start your journey to a Desired Outcome! (I will take you to your "Restore Point" in Module V of this program).

Now I'm going to ask you to describe in your own words the experiences, influences, conditioning and exploitation that shaped your *evolved identity*. This is probably the first time you ever *consciously* explored your *evolved identity!*

Yet this is the *identity* that you project onto others.

STAGE II – Projected Identity

In STAGE II you take your *evolved identity* (which you mistakenly *perceive* as your True Identity and *project* this *evolved identity* onto everyone you connect or come into contact with! This is the stage where most of you will *default* on achieving the RESULTS you're looking for.

Can you see how others see you? Not unless you're psychic or have a way to see *through* the "Mirror of Perception"! Nevertheless, you must find a way to make sure that you *project* the right image in order to achieve the Desired Outcome you're after! Everything from this point on is *focused* on having you *project* the right image.

STAGE III – Perceived Identity

This Stage may be the most *uncomfortable* for you. It removes your personal *control* over your identity and puts it squarely in the hands of those who define and characterize you! The reality is that you don't create your own *identity*, nor do you get to define who you are. "Who you are" is strictly an outcome of your *perceived identity* over which you have little or no control!

But here's the good news!

Over the balance of this program, you're going to learn how to:
- Change the *perception of "Who You Are"*
- Create the *perception you desire!*

Once you create the *perception you desire*, you can *project that perception* and positively influence the way others define and characterize you. You will be able to *influence your perceived identity* in a powerful and positive way!

And in turn, this new *perceived identity* will merge with your *evolved identity* and create a . . . .

STAGE IV – Merged Identity

With this *Signature Program*, you will learn how to transition from your *evolved identity* to a new identity that merges the *perceived identity* that others now define and characterize you by and with the *evolved identity* that you started off with! This "merger of identities" produces a brand new *identity* that I refer to as the *unified identity*.

This *merged identity* will become STAGE I of your next "Cycle of Identity"

True Identity – What is it and why is it important?

As you can see from the diagram at the top of this module, the 4 Stages of the "Circle of Identity" all revolve as planets around a star.

Your TRUE IDENTITY!

Your True Identity is your *spiritual identity*. It cannot be put on display, yet it is omnipresent. There are many different ways to describe True Identity, from the spiritual realm to the outer reaches of quantum physics! Since this book is about developing your new *Persona* and not trying to explain abstract of adjunct theories, I will not dwell on the spiritual significance of True Identity, except to point out that is very much in existence. And while we cannot see it or touch it physically, we all experience its omnipresence on occasion.

In Module VII, I go into great detail on the significance of True Identity, but for now you need to be aware of its existence!

While there are many ways in which we can experience the existence of True Identity, it is most commonly felt when there is a *clash* between True Identity (which is spiritual in nature) and *perceived identity* (which is often a creation of EGO). When such a clash occurs, we experience anxiety and stress. Severe clashes can create feelings of extreme discomfort or even depression.

When we experience these symptoms, our True Identity is signaling us that the path we chose is the wrong path, the choices we made are the wrong choices and the decisions we took are the wrong decisions!

Our True Identity acts as a *safeguard* against any *perceived identity* that is not in alignment with our core values, our inherent personality traits and our connection with our Creator.

◆   ◆   ◆   ◆   ◆

Signposts:

1. Which factors played a role the creating of your *evolved identity*?

_____

_____

_____

_____

_____

2. How would you describe your *evolved identity*?

_____

_____

_____

_____

_____

3. How would you describe your *projected identity*?

_____

_____

_____

_____

_____

4. How would you describe your *perceived identity*?

_____

_____

_____

_____

_____

5. How would you describe your *merged identity*?

_____

_____

_____

_____

_____

6. How would you describe your *True Identity*?

_____

_____

_____

_____

_____

MODULE III

Different MASKS for Different TASKS

Outline

- At this time, you will likely have little or no CONTROL over your *projected* or *perceived identity*, yet that *identity* is responsible for the situation you are in!
- Your *identity* is (in large measure) created and formulated by your INFLUENCERS.
- INFLUENCERS are people who made an impact on you in the past, or will make an impact in the future.
- In order to create RESULTS, you must break free from the "Cycle of Identity", interrupt the process of *perception* and take CONTROL over your *identity*.
- You can take control over your *identity* by wearing a "Social MASK" that you "display "to others.
- This "Social MASK" is your new *Persona*.

If you don't control the way in which you are perceived, your *identity* will be at the mercy of those who *judge, label, define and characterize* you. In order to achieve the RESULTS you are looking for, you must display a "Social MASK" for the *"person who would be successful"*.

The person *you* must become!

And then you must create a new *Persona* for that person!

> *We all wear different masks for different tasks!*
> *The mask is our Persona.*
> *What lies behind the mask*
> *and gives it its unique characteristics,*
> *is our Personality*
>
> ~Allan N. Mulholland

In the previous module, I introduced you to the "Cycle of Identity". Every stage of this cycle is in some way responsible for the situation you are in, or is hindering your ability to achieve a Desired Outcome.

Much of what happens in the "Cycle of Identity" is determined by your *projected identity* and *perceived identity*. They will in turn shape your *unified identity* and *evolved identity!*

There is however one very important common denominator that applies to all four stages of the "Cycle of Identity!

LACK OF CONTROL!

You don't have any *control* over the outcome of each stage! You are at the mercy of *perceptions* that have either been created *by* you or *for* you!

In STAGE I (Evolved Identity), your *perceived identity* was shaped by a lifetime of experiences, influences, conditioning and exploitation. You had little or no control over these events!

In STAGE II (Projected Identity), you projected your *identity* onto others. And since this *projected identity* was largely the result of the *evolved identity* from STAGE I, you had little or no control over the *impressions* you created when you connected with others. *"What you see is what you get"* can have a devastating effect on the outcome of STAGE II!

In STAGE III (Perceived Identity), you are being *classified* by whatever impressions you created in STAGE II. In fact, your *perceived identity* is a random compilation of *impressions and perceptions* that the *INFLUENCERS* in your life will use to *judge, label, define and characterize* you.

And who are these *INFLUENCERS?*

They are the people that play an important role in your personal or professional life. INFLUENCERS are:

- Your employers (current or prospective)
- Your relationships (current or prospective)
- Your business associates (current or prospective)
- Your family

- Your financial contacts (current or prospective)
- Your social contacts (current or prospective)

These *INFLUENCERS* are critical to the successful achievement of your Desired Outcome and for you to be at the *mercy* of their impressions and perceptions is an untenable situation!

In STAGE IV (Merged Identity), you will adopt the (often negative) *perceptions* that *INFLUENCERS* have about you and assimilate them into a new form of *self-perception* that now becomes the basis for the start of the next "Cycle of Identity".

You need to BREAK THIS CYCLE!

At some point during the "Cycle of Identity", you are going to *interrupt* the cycle, and take *control* over the outcome!

But at which stage of the cycle do you *interrupt* it *and how do you take control?*

This is the most *fundamental* part of this book. This is where *you* start to develop your new *Persona* that will ultimately lead you to your Desired Outcome!

Since every stage of the "Cycle of Identity" is influenced by the previous one, the stage you are going to interrupt is STAGE I (Evolved Identity). You are going to *discard* your evolved identity and replace it with a new *Persona* that is modeled after the *"person who would be successful"*!

Your previously *evolved identity* is headed for the dumpster!

In its place will be a brand new *Persona for the person who would be successful in achieving the Desired Outcome you are looking for!*

And who exactly *is* this person?

- It is the *future PROJECTION* of your *identity.*
- It is the *future PERCEPTION* of your *identity.*

It is the "MASK" you must wear to take control over your *projected and perceived identity!* This "MASK" will NOT create a *deceptive identity!* It must be completely aligned with your True Identity, or it will not be effective. If the "MASK" is not aligned with your inherent *personality traits* it will not create your Desired Outcome! The "MASK" simply represents your *identity* that is now *purposefully and powerfully projected* onto the INFLUENCERS who will ultimately define and characterize you!

But since you will take *control* (to a large extent) over your *projected identity*, you will be able to have a positive *impact* on the *perceived identity* that will be created for you by your INFLUENCERS!

So what is this "MASK" that is so essential to your ability to alter and control your *perceived identity* and create a new *Persona* for the *person who would be successful in achieving the Desired Outcome you are looking for!*

• What would be the *Persona* of the *person who would be successful* in attracting the right partner to build an ideal relationship with?

• What would be the *Persona* of the *person who would be successful* in landing that dream job or promotion?

21

• What would be the *Persona* of the *person who would be successful* in achieving your Desired Outcome?

For the answer to that question, we need to go back in history! It was the classic Greek theatre of 500 BC that relied heavily on "MASKS" to define and develop its characters on stage. The Greek term for "MASK" is *Persona* and the ancient Greek performers deployed their masks to convey to the audience their emotions and character traits. The Greek theatre mask was therefore the transformational link between the actor and his character or *Stage Persona*.

Altering and controlling your *projected and perceived identity* uses a similar principle, except that it reverses the analytical process. For example, if it's a relationship you want to develop with someone, you must first create an *identity* for the person who would be the likely candidate to develop that relationship.

This will be your new *PERSONA.*

You may ask: "Is this new *Persona* a genuine representation or a deceptive imitation of such a person? Am I being honest to my new partner? Isn't it better to 'just be myself'? It sounds as if I'm impersonating someone I'm not!"

My answer is always the same: "Your new *Persona* will never change your inherent personality traits."

"Yes, you will be a different person, but you will never be another person. Your *Persona* is always aligned with your core values and beliefs!

In the vernacular used throughout this book, I use the following definitions:

Persona

- The character that you project you're your INFLUENCERS. This is your "Social MASK"!

While the temptation to substitute the word 'personality' in place of 'persona' will at times be seductive and even feel appropriate, I draw a clear distinction between the two interpretations. The term 'personality' will be defined as follows:

Personality

- The sum total of your physical, mental, emotional and social characteristics that are uniquely yours.

Your *personality* gives your *Persona* that uniqueness that makes it different from anyone else. So while a *Persona* will change a *perceived identity*, your *personality* remains true to your own unique values and characteristics. A new *Persona* does not create an imitations of someone else. It crafts a uniquely qualified individual.

> *Our Persona is what defines us;*
> *Our personality is what distinguishes us.*
>
> ~Allan N. Mulholland

In Module IV you start to create your new *Persona*! This is the *perceived identity* that will be under your control and will be modeled after the *person who would be successful in achieving the RESULTS you are looking for!*

Signposts:

1. Why is it important to have *control* over the way your identity is *projected and perceived?*

_____

_____

_____

_____

_____

2. Who are your primary INFLUENCERS?

_____

_____

_____

_____

_____

3. Why do you need to break your "Cycle of Identity"?

_____

_____

_____

_____

_____

4. How would you describe a "Social MASK" (Persona)?

_____

_____

_____

_____

_____

MODULE IV
Creating a New Persona

Outline

- You identify seven essential elements that make up your new *Persona*.
- Behaviors will bring structure to your life. It will restore order out of chaos.
- You identify five patterns of social interaction that will allow you to successfully integrate with those whose approval and positive influence is an essential element in achieving your objectives!
- You must embrace the positive, neutralize the negative and eliminate the toxic INFLUENCERS.
- You have begun the process of programming and conditioning your new *Persona* to become the *"person who would be successful"*. You do this by internalizing every element of this *Persona* in terms of emotions, behavioral patterns, sociology, language, environment, psychology and physiology.

In this module, you bring together the seven elements that are required for the development of your new *Persona*. These are the elements that make up the profile of the *"person who would be successful"*.

The person you have to become!

When you stand in front of the "Mirror of Perception", you will see your image reflected. Every detail of your physical being is reproduced by the mirror and this image is only limited by the size, dimensions and proximity to the mirror. However if the mirror is warped, the image becomes distorted. If the mirror is chipped or cracked, the image becomes fragmented. A flawed mirror no longer reflects the image that you wish to portray.

When you project your *self-perception* onto others, it will reflect this image in much the same way. The image you project onto your INFLUENCERS will be that of a full-length mirror. It must accurately display every detail of the image you intend to project. A true reflection of the way you want to be perceived.

- A reflection of achievement and success.
- A reflection of love and devotion.
- A reflection of valor and determination.
- A reflection of your best!

But if you have a *self-perception* that is limiting or even sabotaging your chances of achieving success, it is as if you're standing in front of a warped and shattered mirror.

You become the mirror image of a distorted and fractured self.

It is crucial to your success that you project the proper *self-perception*. By creating a new *Persona*, you are in fact creating a new *self-perception*. Your *self-perception* becomes the personification of your *self-worth* and your *self-esteem*. A positive projection of your *self-perception* will become your trajectory to success. And since your *self-perception* will be permanently anchored to your new *Persona*, it's imperative that you assemble all the essential elements required to design and develop a *Persona* that is truly representative of the *self-perception* you wish to portray.

Your *Persona* is of your own creation. It is the result of a creative collaboration between you and the *"person who would be successful"*. It is consciously crafted by a vision of *"the person who would be successful"* and subconsciously molded by your behavioral patterns, emotional traits, environmental circumstances and psychological and physiological conditioning.

As with any creative endeavor - whether it's a musical composition, a literary manuscript, a marble sculpture or an oil painting – the true value lies in the interpretation of the creation. The interpretation of your *Persona* is therefore paramount to your eventual success and the results you want to achieve.

When you hear a song or a symphony, it can either stir up a plethora of emotions that leaves you in a state of pure joy and ecstasy, or it can resonate with feelings of discord and dissonance. A book can open your imagination to infinite possibilities or it can poison your mind with the venom of the author's pen. A sculpture or painting can extol the beauty of its imagery or the dark despair of the artist's soul.

Your new *Persona* works very much the same way. The unique qualities of your *Persona* are accentuated by the equally unique interpretive values that will be assigned to it. No two people will interpret your *Persona* in exactly the same way. Not everyone will define or characterize your *Persona* in a positive way and as a result, they will reject a meaningful relationship or partnership with you. No matter how popular or visually stunning a movie is, there will always be those who will fail to appreciate it. No matter how profound the message in a book or poem, there will always be those whose minds will remain closed. No matter how vividly a painter creates a canvas of contrasting colors, there will always be those who will be critical of its compositional complexities.

It is therefore the definition or interpretation given to your *Persona* that gives it its significance and omnipotence. It can dramatically change each and every aspect of your life. It is the power that will allow you to be successful at anything you do!

Let's examine how your new *Persona* will change the way in which you need to be defined and characterized in the areas of:

1.   Career and Business
2.   Family and Relationships
3.   Health and Fitness
4.   Finance
5.   Personal Growth
6.   Spiritual Growth

You will need to chart a new course of action for each of these six categories. You will need to find a new direction in order for you to thrive and not just survive in your chosen career or business. You will need to strengthen your commitment to your family and loved ones and test your resolve to making these relationships your anchor of choice rather than an albatross around your neck. You will need to respect your body as the temple of your soul by cleansing and nurturing your physical entity. You must re-examine your values and beliefs and find your moral compass to become a leader that others can follow and rely upon.

Personal wealth and financial freedom are the foundations for your physical independence.   Your connection with your Creator will foster interdependence with your spirituality and the Universe.

There has never been a greater need for awareness and urgency to make these paradigm shifts! Your mindset must be focused on a quest to thrive and 'be alive'. You must become the *"person who would be successful"*!

Your new *Persona* will allow you to become that person!

You need to bring together the seven elements that are required for the future development of your new *Persona*. These are the elements that make up the *profile* of the *"person who would be successful"*.

The person you need to become!

These elements are:

1. **The *emotional patterns* of such a person.**

First, you're going to expose the *emotional* patterns of the *"person who would be successful"*! These *emotional patterns* must become part of your new *Persona*. Your new *Persona* must be full of fresh and vibrant emotions that belong to the *"person who would be successful"*! These emotions must create the will and passion to achieve any RESULTS you are looking to achieve!

So what kind of emotions would run through such a person's veins? Of the dozens of emotions we all experience on a regular basis, think of three (or more) that you can attribute to *"the person who would be successful"*.

Answer the following three questions for each of these emotions:

- How would you describe the emotion?
- Why is this emotion important to your new *Persona*?
- How will this emotion be different from the way you felt before?

It is important that your new *Persona* has empowering emotions. Your RESULTS will depend on them!

2. The *behavioral patterns* of such a person.

To achieve any Desired Outcome, you need order. Without order, there is chaos. Perhaps you are no stranger to chaos. Perhaps your life is in a state of chaos and confusion right now. Perhaps that's why you are reading this book!

Life can be hectic. For many of us it is a constant balancing act. We have commitments to our family. Our children need our attention. Our work is getting more demanding all the time. We want to stay healthy and fit. We must be careful about our diet. It's so easy to get overwhelmed. We all need order in our lives.

Your behavioral patterns will guard against chaos and overwhelm. Remember, it is never the situation that you're in which causes chaos. It is the way in which you react to the situation. It is the way in which you interpret the problem. It is the way in which you deal with the issues. Your reactions and interpretations are governed by your behavioral patterns. Now is the time to restore order in your life.

Your new *Persona* must have the behavioral patterns of *"the person who would be successful"*. Whatever your goals or objectives, *if they are a MUST*, your behavioral patterns will mimic your commitment to achieve success! Your new *Persona* must establish discipline and order so that you can succeed. These behavioral patterns must be enshrined in your new *Persona*. If it's a new relationship you want, the way in which you behave will determine whether the outcome will be successful. Your behavioral patterns will be crucial during a job interview. They will guide a new business venture. They will create a level of authenticity for your relationship with your Creator.

More than anything else, your behavior mirrors your *Persona*. Your positive behavior is the first line of defense when others define and characterize you. Inappropriate behavior (by that I mean behavioral patterns that are not in consort with your goal or objective) will immediately cast a shadow over your *Persona!*

Of all the patterns that make up your new *Persona*, your behavior is often the most visible and transparent.

I want you to identify five behaviors which your new *Persona* must display in order to create RESULTS. What must your behavior be like and how does it differ from past behavioral patterns?

Create a clear image in your mind about the RESULT you want to achieve. Next, create a "vision" of the RESULT, while you're in the 'character' of the *"person who would be successful"*. How would this person behave? How would such behavior be *perceived*?

Identify five behaviors that will set you apart and will allow you to achieve the RESULTS you're looking for!

- How would you describe these behaviors?
- Why are these behaviors particularly important to your new *Persona?*
- How are these behaviors different from the way you behaved before?

3. The *sociological patterns* of such a person.

Now that your new *Persona* has the ability to create order out of chaos with the appropriate behavioral patterns, it's time for you to shift your attention to your *sociology!*

Your new *Persona* alters your habits and characteristics, until they are perfectly aligned with the goals and objectives for which your *Persona* is created and the RESULTS you intend to achieve.

The patterns of your sociology carry within them the ability for your new *Persona* to function in consort with your personality traits. Your new *Persona* must align itself with the patterns of sociological belief and the actions of those with whom you will need to interact. That means that your new *Persona* must share the values of those with whom you wish to establish a relationship. This may include your employer, your partner, your business clientele, your church congregation, your support groups or any other social group with which you need to interact.

The social patterns of your new *Persona* must match the ways in which you're expected to behave in certain social circles, whether this is at work or during social events. Your new *Persona* must be able to play the role you're expected to play as a result of the position you hold in society or the situation you are in. How society defines your new *Persona* will be determined by the "Social MASK" that you are going to display.

Identify five patterns of social interaction that will allow your new *Persona* to successfully integrate with those whose approval and positive influence are essential elements for achieving RESULTS!

- How would you describe these Social Patterns?
- Why are these Social Patterns of particular importance to your new *Persona*?
- How are these new Social Patterns different from your previous one?

4. The *linguistic patterns* of such a person.

Your words are by far the most powerful and direct way to communicate your message. The English language has the greatest number of defined and catalogued words of any language in the world, followed by German and with French as a distant third. But out of the approximately 250,000 words contained in the Oxford dictionary, the average person uses less than 20,000.

Words are like the colors on a canvas or the notes in a musical composition. The correct mixture of colors makes a painting look vibrant and alive. A clash in colors is disturbing to the beholder. The sequence of a set of musical notes can create a beautiful, rich and harmonious melody or it can invoke feelings of dissonance and discord.

Combining the right words on the pallet of communication can produce powerful strokes to underscore a message. Using words incorrectly can leave the message impotent and confusing.

Your new *Persona* needs the ability to communicate *effectively*. This applies not only to your choice of words, but also to the delivery of your speech, your voice intonations and the subtle nuances in your language patterns. There may even be the occasional silence.

Indeed, the power of your new *Persona* is manifested by the words you use.

5. The *environmental influences* on such a person.

You cannot eliminate all of the environmental influences that can affect your new *Persona*. Some of these influences will be beyond your control. But similar to the pH level in the soil of a garden, you can neutralize the environmental effects on your new *Persona*.

Too much acid from one source can be balanced by the alkaline you receive from another. If some family members cannot identify with your new *Persona* and pour acid on your fertile soil, you must turn to other relatives or friends to garner their support and restore a healthy pH balance. The acid only stings if you connect with it. Your *perception* of someone's negative attitude can give the acidity its potency, or it can be neutralized on the spot. That choice is always up to you. You may not be able to change parts of your environment, but you can certainly minimize its impact on your new *Persona*.

However, you must never allow toxic waste to be dumped in your back yard. *Not under any circumstances!* If someone is out to destroy your new *Persona*, that person must be immobilize by removing him/her from your list of INFLUENCERS! Criticism and skepticism may be acidic, but they can be neutralized. Constructive criticism may even prove to be alkaline in disguise. But if someone openly attacks your new *Persona* with the intent to destroy it, that person must be removed from your "sphere of influence". Toxic waste is poisonous and the acidity will destroy your new *Persona* or render it ineffective.

Thinks about the people and circumstances that were a major influence in your past and will likely continue to be an INFLUENCER in the future. I suggest that you select three or more individuals that have, and will continue to have a positive influence on you. We will call these the ALKALINE INFLUENCERS.

Next, select three or more individuals that have, and will continue to have a negative influence on you. We will call these the ACIDIC INFLUENCERS.

Finally, select three or more individuals that have, and will continue to have a poisonous influence on you. Call these the TOXIC INFLUENCERS.

Next, you'll examine the psychology and physiology of your new *Persona*. These elements determine your ability and determination to achieve RESULTS!

6. The *psychological characteristics* of such a person.

Psychology is an integral part of your new *Persona*. It will become its guiding force. There are many qualities that can be ascribed to the *"person who would be successful"*, but here are some of the most important ones:

- Control
- Influence
- Contribution
- Growth
- Responsibility
- Trust
- Attitude
- Vision
- Self-esteem
- Respect
- Humility
- Gratefulness
- Courage
- Motivation
- Accountability
- Personal Development
- Discipline
- Inspiration
- Optimism
- Empathy

Select the 5 qualities that you think are the most important to fit the psychology of the *"person who would be successful"*!

- How would you describe these qualities?
- Why are these qualities of particular importance to your new *Persona*?
- How are these qualities different from their previous one?

7. The physiological characteristics of such a person.

If your body language is *out of alignment* with your new *Persona*, it's time to sit up straight and take notice! Your deportment or the way you use your physiology is usually an accurate depiction of your attitude. That is certainly not a unique assessment. The way we feel is usually reflected in the way we stand, the way we look, the way we sit or shake hands. So how would you describe the physiology of the *"person who would be successful"?* Is that person's *stance* different from yours? Is that person's *appearance* different from yours? Does that person seem to sit up straighter? Would that person have a firmer handshake? How is the *demeanor* of such a person different from yours?

Would that person be fitter, have more energy, eat healthier, have a better balanced diet and take better care of his/her appearance?

Would that person handle stress better? How would that person resolve issues? Through negotiation or confrontation?

How would you describe your current physiology?

Imagine yourself as the *"person who would be successful"* and think of how that would feel!

How would that affect your self-esteem, your actions, the way you behave, the way you conduct yourself, the way you dress, the way you would greet people, the way you would handle your job, the way you would deal with your family and children, the way you would make decisions, the way you would take responsibility for your actions, the way you would change your life or improve the quality of your life.

How would you see your physiology change in terms of your physical expressions and capabilities, gestures, stance, breathing, presence and so on?

What will becoming the *"person who would be successful"* means to you and why is it so important that these 7 essential elements are enshrined in your new *Persona*! You must be very specific this time. It is extremely important to have your new *Profile* connect with the *"person who would be successful"*. It will be crucial to the long-term success of your new *Persona* that you have an absolutely clear understanding of *who, what and why* this person is!

Next, I want you to take two action steps in each of the following six areas and make these a part of your new *Persona!* What MUST you achieve with your new *Persona* in the areas of:

- Your body? (health, weight, fitness, energy, diet, etc.)
- Your family? (children, spouse, parents, siblings, etc.)
- Your business or career? (opportunities, advancement, change, etc.)
- Your friends and relationships? (lover, companion, etc.)
- Your finances? (more income, less debt, better investments)
- Your spirituality? (stronger beliefs, closer connection with your Creator or the Universe)

Can you see yourself as the *"person who would be successful"*? Focus on these concepts and watch your new *Persona* take shape!

◆ ◆ ◆ ◆ ◆

Signposts:

1. Do you experience mostly positive or negative emotions on a regular basis? Can you name these emotions?

_____

_____

_____

_____

_____

2. Which types of behavior will bring structure to your life? What behaviors are creating chaos right now?

_____
_____
_____
_____
_____

3. How would you describe your role _in_ and the value you bring _to_ society?

_____
_____
_____
_____
_____

4. Do you consider yourself a good communicator? How could you improve on your communication skills?

_____
_____
_____
_____
_____

5. How would you describe the environment that you live in? Is it mainly positive, negative or toxic?

_____
_____
_____
_____
_____

6. What does leadership mean to you personally?

_____
_____
_____
_____
_____

MODULE V

Finding Your Restore Point

<u>**Outline**</u>
- You are going to select a Restore Point from where you'll start to put your new *Persona* together.
- You will make a list of the 'wrong choices' you made since the last time you visited your *Restore Point*, so that you won't make the same choices again.
- You make a list of all the external influences that have prevented you from achieving success in the Past.
- You identify and acknowledge the fears and emotions that have shaped your *identity* in the Past!
- You identify the INFLUENCERS that can threaten or destroy your new *Persona*.

<u>**Objective**</u>
In this module, I will take you to a *Restore Point* from where you can follow a different path to your Desired Outcome. A *Restore Point* from where you will start to develop your new *Persona!*

I have never met a client for whom I could not find a *Restore Point!* A *Restore Point* from where they will start to develop their new *Persona!* This is the point in your *Past* where you chose to follow a certain direction on life's journey.

At some point in our lives, we all arrive at a certain crossroads where we must make a decision:

Do we turn left or right?

Sometimes we choose a partner and ask that person to join us on our journey. But what if we chose the wrong partner?

Sometimes we commit to a career path based on our education or our family's expectations. But what if we're unhappy with our career choice?

Perhaps we opened up a business, only to find that it is not profitable or even viable.

What if we were seduced into believing that drugs or alcohol are the antidote to our pain?

Maybe we follow a faith that is no longer meeting our spiritual needs.

We can never go back into our Past and change it! But we *can* go back to that intersection and start a new journey in a different direction. We can go back to that *Restore Point* and turn right where we once turned left!

When I take you to your *Restore* Point, you'll experience a sense of familiarity. You've been there before! This is déjà vu.

The intersection will look different! A lot of time has passed! The landscape around the intersection will have changed. The options that were open to you in the Past will now be different. The choices you were given then may no longer be available.

The fork in the road will look different from the way you remember it! But old choices have been replaced by new choices that are available now.

The allure of a new beginning is beckoning you. New opportunities are waiting. All you need to do is make some new choices!

The last time you were at the cross-roads, you made certain choices. These choices did not deliver your desired results. So how can you be sure that this time, you will make the right decisions?

The answer to that question depends on who is making the decisions!

Will it be your *identity* from the past or your new *Persona*?

To prepare for the journey back to your *Restore Point,* you need to relax and clear your thoughts!

May I suggest that you find a quiet place to meditate? A favorite spot! Maybe you could go for a walk! As you meditate, revisit a time in the past when you had dreams and aspirations. Go back to a time when you had goals and ambitions. When you wanted to be different from the *judgments, labels, definitions and characterizations* that are now part of your *perceived identity.*

Go back to that time, so you can *replant* the seeds of your True Identity that have long since been trampled on and suffocated. Go back to that *Restore Point* where the seeds of your True Identity are still dormant and waiting to be re-planted.

Now close your eyes and create a mental image of your *Restore Point.* Perhaps you can write a description, draw a picture or a map, or take a photograph and label it *"My Restore Point".* Take a few minutes to come up with the right imagery. It's from here that you will "grow" your new *Persona!*

Weeding the Restore Point

OK, it's time for you to roll up your sleeves and put on the garden gloves. Your *Restore Point* has been neglected for a very long time and now it's overgrown with weeds.

Even the evergreens that are the remnants of your past achievements need some pruning and the colorful plants and flowers that form your "Equity of the Past" are barely visible in this jungle of untamed overgrowth.

The "weeds" at your *Restore Point* represent all the things that are wrong about your *projected and perceived identity.* These weeds must be extracted from the *Restore Point* and discarded one-by-one.

Weeds of doubt, inferiority and low self-esteem have no place at your *Restore Point*. They suck up all the nutrients from the rich soil, leaving it barren and unproductive.

This is your wasteland of past failings and misfortunes.

Make sure that you don't just skim the surface with the string of your weed-eater. This may give the illusion of a fresh start, but unless you pull out those weeds by the roots, they will re-appear and your future achievements will be stunted and stagnated.

These weeds are not all the same.

Some are small and easy to pull out.

Others seem to have long roots and are hard to remove.

Just before you discard the "weeds" of your *perceived identity* and toss them into the compost bin, you need to *catalogue* them.

These "weeds" represent the misconceptions you have about *"Who You Are"*.

They represent the choices you made that steered you in the wrong direction.

I prefer not to think of these as "mistakes", but rather as "wrong choices". I believe that everything happens for a reason, so there are no mistakes.

At this point, you should be able to identify three (or more) "weeds" that you have discarded.

Once you have pulled out the "weeds", it's time to clean up the rest of your *Restore Point*.

Get your shovel and wheelbarrow ready!

And drink plenty of water!

This will be heavy work!

Removing Rocks & Debris

The "weeds" you pulled at your *Restore Point* represent the *internal blockages* that prevented you from pursuing your dreams and goals in the Past. These are the misconceptions and poor choices that steered you in the wrong direction.

The "rocks" that are scattered about your *Restore Point* are the external roadblocks that stopped you from achieving your goals and living the life you desire. These "rocks" were always a part of the landscape, so you ignored them! They are a part of your environment. This would include your family, your upbringing, your education, the places you lived, the country you were born in and any social or religious influences you were exposed to.

Basically, all the influences over which you had no control in the past but are now in a position to remove or relocate. Yes, some of the "boulders" are just too heavy to remove all together, but with some effort they can be relocated to an area where they can no longer inhibit the growth of your new *Persona*.

The debris that is strewn about the *Restore Point* is the rubbish that you collected over the years and allowed to pile up. These are the negative influences that you permitted to be dumped at your *Restore Point* by INFLUENCERS who were just looking for a place to get rid of their personal garbage. These are the labels that people have attached to you, the negative perceptions they created about you, the ways in which they put you down, diminished your value and importance, made you feel inferior, used you for their personal benefit and abused you for their personal significance!

Let's get out the wheelbarrow and remove three (or more) "rocks" that have disempowered you in the Past but can now be removed from your *Restore Point*. Don't forget to label these "rocks" and catalogue them for future reference!

Are there any "boulders" that will always be at the *Restore Point* because they're impossible to remove, such as a health issue or a financial obligation? Let's move them to a place from where their impact on your new *Persona* can be managed and controlled!

Finally, let's clean up the debris. List three (or more) items that have held you back in the Past, but are now destined for the dumpster.

Whew! Mission accomplished! Your *Restore Point* looks much neater now.

Tilling the Soil

Let's get out the spade and start digging deep into your Past. This time you're not looking for rocks or debris. This time you're not killing weeds. This time you want to turn all your negative conditioning upside down.

You're going to unearth the demons from your Past. The beliefs that you hold about yourself and your environment.

This is the *acidity* in the soil that has been allowed to accumulate over the years and that has *stunted and stagnated* your personal growth! How do you feel about yourself? What negative emotions are harboring below the surface? What are you afraid of?

Were you popular as a child? Were you shy? How did you do in school? How was your relationship with your parents?

Your *perceived identity* was likely cultivated in the same soil that is now a part of your *Restore Point*. If the soil is too acidic or too alkaline, your new *Persona* will not develop properly. If the soil lacks the proper nutrients, your new *Persona* will not reach its potential. If you don't water your new *Persona*, it will dehydrate. Give it too much water and it will drown. Too much shade will make your new *Persona* shy and demure. Too much light will make it boisterous and arrogant.

A *Persona* that is warmed by the sun, yet cooled by the breeze will grow into a beautiful arbor. Give it the right nutrients and sufficient water and your *Persona* will grow strong and independent. So you need to till the soil at your *Restore Point* in order to expose all the toxicity in the ground and allow the earth below to become refreshed and revitalized!

I want you to think back and start digging for significant events that made an impact on your life. Now list the three (or more) most important ones.

What are some of the fears you had in the Past that may still impact you today?

What are some of the emotions you felt in the Past and are still dealing with today?

Protecting the Restore Point

Your *Restore Point* needs protection from the elements that may want to destroy your new *Persona*, the parasites that may want to invade it and the unscrupulous INFLUENCERS that may want to steal or sabotage it.

So what are the elements that could destroy your *Persona*? They are the environmental hazards that you are constantly subjected to. The environment that you live and work in can be harmful to your new *Persona*. And that environment starts with your immediate family. A spouse or partner can create a nurturing environment for you to grow in. But he/she can also suffocate you psychologically or torture you emotionally.

Your family can believe in you or belittle you. They can support you or suppress you. They can elevate you to new heights or send you spiraling down. They can push you over the top or push you over the edge!

The parasites of society live of the avails of achievers and will suck the lifeblood out of your new *Persona*. Once your *Persona* has been invaded by parasites, it will suffer from a terminal illness that can only be eradicated by the creation of a new and uninfected *Persona*.

The third type of intruder into your *Restore Point* is the unscrupulous INFLUENCER. While success is openly admired and publicly lauded, it is often secretly resented and feared. In a society where mediocrity is the standard by which much of our personal performance is measured, your new *Persona* may be discomforting for many.

Your new *Persona* will be extremely vulnerable during its formative days. You must guard against foreign invaders and environmental hazards.

Your new *Persona* will be uniquely yours. No two people are alike. Therefore, the challenges and obstacles your new *Persona* will face are also unique.

Identify three (or more) INFLUENCERS who could hurt your new *Persona* while it is still in its infancy and most vulnerable.

Next, list three (or more) environmental hazards (negative social influences from work, church, community, colleagues, etc.) that could hurt your new *Persona*.

Now that you've found a *Restore Point* from where you will start to develop your new *Persona*, it's time to create a *Profile* for the *"person who would be successful"*.

A *Profile* for your new *Persona* that will be modeled after this person!

A *Persona Profile!*

◆   ◆   ◆   ◆   ◆

Signposts:

1. How did you decide on a Restore Point? How far back did you go? What are you hoping to find there?

_____

_____

_____

_____

2. What are some of the "wrong choices" you've made in the past? How will you try to avoid making poor choices for the future?

_____

_____

_____

_____

_____

3. What are some of the negative influences that have prevented you from achieving success in the past?

_____

_____

_____

_____

4. Are there any occurrences, fears or emotions from the past that are still effecting you today?

_____

_____

_____

_____

_____

5. Who are the INFLUENCER that can harm your new Persona?

_____

_____

_____

_____

6. What are some of the personal "demons" that you've "unearthed" in this Module?

_____

_____

_____

_____

_____

MODULE VI

Creating a Persona Profile

Outline

- For you to be in full alignment with the *"person who would be successful"*, you must first align your new *Persona* with a *profile* of such a person.
- There are two types of leadership that are part of your *Persona Profile*:
  - Internal Leadership, and
  - External Leadership.
- There are two fundamental qualities inherent in the *"person who would be successful"*. They are:
  1. The *desire to achieve*, which is similar to an *emotion* and therefore *inspired.*
  2. The *ability to achieve*, which is based on skill sets and expertise and therefore *acquired.*
- Society *conditions* us to accept 'External Leadership" from those who are our INFLUENCERS. But without the guidance of the 'Leader within', these 'External Leaders' simply promote the values of the institutions they represent.
- Leadership is not determined by leadership *skills*, but by leadership *wisdom.*

In this module, you will align your new *Persona* with that of the *"person who would be successful"* by modeling their *Profile.*

Creating a Persona Profile from the Inside Out

In the previous module, you learned about the seven elements of your *Persona*. They are:
1. Emotional patterns
2. Behavioral patterns
3. Sociological patterns
4. Linguistic patterns
5. Environment influences
6. Psychological characteristics
7. Physiological characteristics.

However, your new *Persona* is much more than just a combination of elements in random order. It is about becoming the *"person who would be successful!"*

But it is also about some else. Something even more important than becoming the *"person who would be successful!"* In fact, your new *Persona* will not succeed unless it is a true, genuine, authentic and accurate representation of your True Identity!

You cannot assume someone else's personality traits any more than acquire someone else's natural talents. Personality traits and talents are a part of your DNA. They are what makes you unique!

These personality traits and talents do not need to be acquired. They are inherent. But they can be further developed and refined. They are the "diamonds in the rough" that will only reach their true potential once they've been cut and polished to perfection.

Your new *Persona* will not change your personality traits, *but it will develop them to their highest and best value.*

In this module, you will focus on creating a *profile* for the *"person who would be successful!"* and integrate that *profile* with your new *Persona*. While the profile for the *"person who would be successful!"* will be unique to you, there are certain qualities that are essential to the achievement of success in virtually any category.

It doesn't matter if you want to find a new relationship, start a new career, create a new business, re-connect with family or make a stronger commitment to your faith! It all begins with the *profile* of a LEADER!

All of us are born with the inherent qualities of a Leader. You are no exception! To deny the 'Leader within' is to try to change a personality trait. It cannot be done!

But constant negative *conditioning* can subdue the 'Leader within'. You may have been *conditioned to suppress* the 'Leader within', just as you may have been conditioned to *suppress an emotion*. When emotions and personality traits are suppressed, they may retreat and go dormant but they can never be expunged! Creating a new *Persona Profile* will awaken the comatose 'Leader within' and re-connect you with the *"person who would be successful"*! There are two types of leadership that are part of your *Persona Profile*:
- Internal Leadership, and
- External Leadership.

In order for you to achieve your Desired Outcome, it's important to understand the difference between these two types of Leadership! Both have a valuable role to play. Both are essential to the development of your *Persona Profile*.

Yet, both are vastly different. They are fraternal twins!

If you were not successful in achieving a Desired Outcome, you were likely *conditioned* to fail. This *conditioning* probably took place over an extended period of time and was the result of INFLUENCERS who did not understand or could not care about your true potential.

Before all this conditioning took place however, you were guided by the *'Leader within'* who took you to a cross-roads where you had to make a decision!

Should you turn left or right?

This decision may have been made a long time ago. It may have slipped into obscurity. It may have lost its relevance to your current situation. But it is most likely the decision that ended the role of the *'Leader within'* and started the "Cycle of Identity" that is responsible for the situation you're is in TODAY!

I want you to recall in as much detail as possible, your personal journey that led you to that cross-roads where you abandoned the 'Leader within' and were swept away by the perpetual "Cycle of Identity". I need to take you back to that cross-roads!

This is your "Restore Point".

Internal Leadership vs External Leadership

External Leaders are 'conditioned' leaders. They are conditioned to accept and represent the philosophies of the corporate, political, military or religious institutions they now lead.

Your *Persona Profile* must be a true, genuine, authentic and accurate representation of the *"person who would be successful"*. That person must be guided by the 'Leader within'. This person is not motivated by ego, but by the ability to achieve RESULTS!

There is nothing wrong with a healthy ego, as long as it is balanced by a sense of genuine humility and gratitude. But if you are creating a *Persona Profile* that will transform you into an 'External Leader', you may want to re-assess your core values and beliefs. If your 'Internal Leader' is in conflict with your 'External Leader', you may find a superficial level of success in the short-term, but the overall quality of your Desired Outcome will be compromised as long as this conflict continues.

Leadership Wisdom

Your *perceived identity* is what defines you. But you are not the ones who created this *perceived identity*. That task belongs to those who come into contact with you. Your INFLUENCERS.

Leadership wisdom influences when, where, how and why that contact takes place. Relentless conditioning may have made it almost impossible for you to tap into that source of wisdom.

Why?

You were *conditioned* to believe that leadership is an acquired skill. You were *conditioned* to believe that leaders are made and not born!

That makes as much sense as suggesting that intelligence is a *learned condition*. The same applies to leadership. Leadership wisdom is not determined by what you learned about being a leader, but by how you apply this knowledge. And that is a consequence of your inborn leadership abilities and your inherent intelligence.

Oh yes, and something else! *Intuition and instinct!*

The Leadership Role

In Module II, we dispelled the myth that *"we are who we are"*. The truth is that we are defined and characterized by our INFLUENCERS.

Your new *Persona* may be part of that process, but it cannot determine its outcome! Ultimately, we don't determine who we are. I trust that the concept of a *perceived identity* is starting to make sense.

The purpose of your new *Persona* is therefore not so much about changing who you are, as it is about changing the *perception* of who you are. Your new *Persona* wants to change the *perception* you project onto your INFLUENCERS!

Your *Persona Profile* must be based on the *"person who would be successful"*. In other word, once you determine what it is you want to achieve, you can create a *profile* for the *"person who would be successful in achieving it"*. Whether that is a relationship with someone special, a new job or career, a new business venture, dealing with a debilitating addiction or a religious connection, your new *Persona* must contain the patterns of emotions, behaviors, sociology and linguistics, as well as the environmental, psychological and physiological characteristics of the *"person who would be successful"*.

But at the same time, your new *Persona* must be a true, genuine, authentic and accurate representation of such a person. And since that person is ultimately a future extension of you and will incorporate all of your personality traits, gifts and talents, it will in fact be a true representation of you!

The Leader in Society

There are only two outcomes of the conditioning that you have been subjected to. The conditioning was either positive or negative. It either encouraged you or discouraged you. It either inflated or deflated your dreams and ambitions.

We can be conditioned for success or failure. However, many people are conditioned to be neither. They are not conditioned to achieve success, for that would mean that they are encouraged to assume a leadership role. Yet, they are not conditioned to fail, because that would make them a burden on society. In fact, they were conditioned to achieve some level of legitimacy in society, so that they can survive in a state of mediocrity that brings them a modicum of comfort but no real satisfaction. And for that privilege, they work hard to provide for their families.

Many of you don't want to be leaders. You may feel inadequate. You may feel that you don't have the talent, the education, the skills, the fortitude or the tenacity to be a leader, because that's how society has conditioned you!

You may feel like the elephant whose leg is tied with a simple piece of string to a flimsy wooden stake in the ground. That elephant will never run away, because at one point he was kept captive by a steel chain that was attached to an immovable tree stump. The elephant's conditioning will last him a lifetime. Your *conditioning* will last until you develop your new *Persona*!

The Family Leader

Of all the segments of society, family is the most important one. Bar none! If you have a family, treat it with the utmost reverence and respect. If you are in the right relationship or married to the right spouse, you are truly blessed. If you have children, biological or adopted, they are a gift from God. Your parents, whether living or deceased, are an eternal testament to your character. Love, respect and honor your family. Without family, nothing is important. Nothing matters!

The family structure is the perfect example of the new convention of Leadership. A family is no different from any other team. Everyone has a role to play and a function to perform. From the youngest child to the oldest grandparent. That role may not be equal in intensity or perceived importance, but it is a role that is unique to the contributor.

You must connect with all members of your family and as often as you can. Exclude no one. Decide today to make the welfare of your family the most important achievement on your list!

The Business Leader

Many of us are still suffering from one of the most severe financial crises in recent memory and the disastrous economic spinoff continues unabated. Corporate leadership has seen its worst failings in years and the continued poor performances of many of our corporate giants is symptomatic of a leadership philosophy that is outdated, outmoded and functionally obsolete. Job dissatisfaction is the malignant cancer on today's work force and corporations and organizations have been dumb, deaf and blind to its impact on productivity.

For those who remember the good ol' days, I have some unsettling news. Nothing ever goes back to the way it was. Many of the jobs that have been lost will not come back. At best, they will be replaced by other jobs. New jobs will be created that never even existed ten years ago.

Perhaps they don't even exist today!

Business leaders are facing a dilemma. They're working from a productivity template that no longer serves as a model for the 21st century. Business leaders are created, molded, transformed, transitioned and conditioned to lead their businesses. As a society, we are in such awe of our corporate leaders that we reward them for their successes and failures. We pay astronomical bonuses to corporate bankers and Wall Street executives for creating the worst financial crisis of the decade, possibly even the last hundred years! If success is a measure of achievement, how do you explain this aberration? You get rewarded for causing a calamity? Go figure!

If you own a business or if you're thinking about starting a new business, you need to create a new *Persona Profile* that is modeled after the *"business leader who would be successful".*

The Spiritual Leader

Regardless of our belief, religion or church affiliation, we all have a value system at our core that is the foundation of our faith. But faith requires guidance. When we lose faith in anything or anyone, it's not that our faith somehow was lost. It simply means that our faith is no longer guided. It is no longer focused.

Our faith is guided by the 'Spiritual Leader' who resides in all of us! Of all the inherent leadership qualities and abilities you possess, the 'Spiritual Leader' is the most important. It is your moral compass and makes the necessary course adjustments and directional changes that will keep you on your chosen path. The 'Spiritual Leader' will keep you focused on your vision, even if that vision is only a spark that has yet to ignite a passion.

If achievement and success are the 'hindsight' of a vision, then faith is the 'foresight' of that vision. And it's the

'Spiritual Leader' who carries you through this period of transition, until your vision becomes reality!

When you develop your new *Persona*, you must align your moral and ethical values with those of your True Identity.

Your faith should be guided by your 'Spiritual Leader'. When that happens, all internal conflict about faith and religion will disappear. Perhaps for the first time in your life, you will achieve true religious freedom!

From Microscope to Telescope

In order for you to achieve your Desired Outcome, you need to see the big picture. You need to take charge and be in control of your life and you must be ready to lead!

Your new *Persona* will give you the opportunity to succeed and achieve your Desired Outcome!

In order for you to see the big picture, you need to step away from the microscope that dissects your goals and achievements into miniscule and disorderly fragmentations. Instead, you must view your future through the powerful lens of a telescope where all relevant matter can be seen as part of one cohesive and orderly Universe.

The telescope through which you will view your future, will reveal the big picture in the following celestial sequence:

1.   With your new *Persona*, you will immediately be connected to the *"person who would be successful"*! You must understand the role you need to play and which "Social MASK" you need to display in order to become

that person! And your new *Persona* will allow you to do so!

2.   You must look at the INFLUENCERS you are connected to and determine their impact. Are these INFLUENCERS able to illuminate your chosen path or is their gravitational pull preventing you from becoming the *"person who would be successful"*?

3.   Are you in a perfectly aligned orbit around the *"person who would be successful"?*

For you to be in full alignment with the *"person who would be successful"*, you must first align your new *Persona* with the seven *elements* that define and characterize such a person! (See Module IV)

To recap, these seven elements are:

1. The *emotional patterns* of such a person.

2. The *behavioral patterns* of such a person.

3. The *sociological patterns* of such a person.

4. The *linguistic patterns* of such a person.

5. The *environmental influences* of such a person.

6. The *psychological characteristics* of such a person.

7. The *physiological characteristics* of such a person.

In other words, you need to create a *profile for the "person who would be successful"* and align that *profile* with the *profile* for your new *Persona!*

Every *Persona* will have its "black hole". It is the space between *perception* and *reality*. The way in which you will be defined and characterized by your INFLUENCERS is based on the *projected and perceived* identity that is being created by your new *Persona*. The difference between a *projected identity* and a *perceived identity* is referred to as the "black hole" of a *Persona*.

The "black hole" in your new *Persona* is not an abyss as one might suspect. It actually contains all the traits and characteristics of *"the person who would be successful"*, but is shielded from the INFLUENCERS because it is enveloped in shadows.

Your new *Persona* requires a source of illumination to shed a light on the "black hole" and to expose its *profile*, so that the INFLUENCERS can see the true composition of the *Persona*. This illumination of your *Persona* takes place when your *Persona Profile* becomes aligned with the *profile for the "person who would be successful"*

Profile of the *"person who would be successful"*

There are two fundamental qualities inherent in the *"person who would be successful"*. The person you must become in order to achieve your Desired Outcome. They are:

1. The *desire to achieve*, which is similar to an *emotion* and therefore *inspired*.

2. The *ability to achieve*, which is based on skill sets and expertise and therefore *acquired*.

You may have the inherent desire to achieve your Desired Outcome but lack the fundamental capabilities until you acquire them! By aligning your *Persona Profile* with that of *"the person who would be successful"*, you will need to acquire all the skill sets required to achieve success.

What will make you capable of achieving your Desired Outcome?

What skill sets will you need to acquire in order to achieve success?

I want you to prepare a detailed list of *qualities* that you must possess in order to create your Desired Outcome.

In preparing this list, try to be *results specific*! In other words, look for *qualities* that will motivate you to achieve results! For example:

• If you want to be a great parent, what will be the skill sets that your new *Persona* must acquire?

• If you want to be a consummate lover, how will your new *Persona* prepare you for that role?

• If you want to be a proficient job applicant, in what ways will your new *Persona* compliment your dazzling résumé?

• If you want to be a motivated career professional, how will your new *Persona* help you climb the ladder of success?

• If you want to be a dedicated health & fitness devotee, what attributes must your new *Persona* display?

• If you want to be a spiritual guide or counselor, what qualities must your new *Persona* have to create that connection with your faith?

Creating a *profile* for your *Persona* is an exercise in triumph over challenge! If you already have the *desire* to create a Desired Outcome, a properly aligned *Persona* will soon give you the ability to achieve results!

Signposts:

1. How would you describe the correlation between your new *Persona* and the profile of *"the person who would be successful"*?

_____

_____

_____

_____

_____

2. Is your new *Persona* fully aligned with *"the person who would be successful"*? What are some of the areas where your new *Persona* is not yet completely aligned?

_____

_____

_____

_____

_____

3. Can you explain in your own words the difference between the *desire to achieve* and the *ability to achieve*?

_____

_____

_____

_____

_____

4. Can you explain in your own words the difference between the *Internal Leadership* and *External Leadership*?

_____

_____

_____

_____

_____

5. What skillsets will you need to become an effective leader? How many of these skillsets do you already possess? Which ones do you still need to acquire?

_____

_____

_____

_____

_____

◆　◆　◆　◆　◆

MODULE VII

Measure of Success

<u>Outline</u>

- The formula for success is based on a set of values that your new *Persona* shares with the *"person who would be successful"*. These values must be a true, genuine, authentic and accurate representation of such a person.
- Success cannot be measured by any conventional standard. It must be measured on an individual basis and aligned with a person's True Identity.
- Lasting success cannot be achieved through deception or fraud. If the *perception* of success hinges on expensive toys and living a lavish lifestyle, you're courting with disaster!
- Success in itself is meaningless unless there is value attached to it. We are not successful if the only beneficiary of our success is us.

In this module, you will align your new *Persona* with the Desired Outcome you want to achieve. This is how you measure your success!

The Formula for Success

You're going to look at success. You're going to find out what success means to you and how it fits in with your *Persona*.

There are as many definitions for success as there are people who wish to define it. Most dictionaries agree on some generic definition of success, such as "the achievement of something desired, planned or attempted".

To me, success is *achieving a Desired Outcome*.

The formula for success is based on a set of values that your new *Persona* shares with the *"person who would be successful"*. These values must be a true, genuine, authentic and accurate representation of such a person.

The person you need to become!

Here are some of the values that are closely aligned with the *profile* of the *"person who would be successful"*!

1 - Be authentic

Success will have little significance, unless it is achieved through the authentic application of the values and principles by which your new *Persona* will be defined.

2 - Make a contribution

Any measure of success increases exponentially with the level of contribution it makes! Achieving success for a self-serving purpose is not in keeping with your *value proposition*.

3 - Create a vision

In order for any achievement to be "desired, planned or attempted", it must first have purpose. Without purpose, there is no need to achieve. The purpose of your achievement is aligned with the vision you have for the achievement. You must know the outcome you're after! You must devise a way to get to that outcome. *You need a vision!*

4 - Have a strategy

You need a roadmap for success. Start off by planning the route and place markers along the way to keep you on track. Watch out for the road blocks and detours. And remember that any good strategy must also have contingencies in place.

5 - Find your passion

> *Success is imminent where passion is evident!*
> ~ Allan N. Mulholland

Passion is the fuel that runs the engine of success. Whatever results you are after, confirm that your passion is at the core of it! Check your fuel gage and make sure you're running on a full tank of passion!

6 - Risk is your lightning rod!

Staying indoors during a storm may provide you with a safe haven, but you will never be struck by the lightning bolt of success.

Success does not come with guarantees, but then neither does life! So take chances and take them often. Sooner or later, they'll be struck by lightning! But until that moment happens . . . . . .

7 - Have faith!

Risk is a seduction!
Chance is an opportunity.
Faith is the difference!

~ Allan N. Mulholland

You should never underestimate the power of faith! It is the one intangible that can turn risk into chance. Always have faith!

8 - Become a 'success environmentalist'

Success only grows in the proper environment. If those around you are a toxic influence on your success, it's time to uproot and relocate. You must be surrounded by those who share your values, goals and objective. With the synergy of a positive environment, your success will be immense!

9 - Actions speak louder than words

Success will remain a lofty illusion, until you actually achieve it! The chances you take today will create the RESULTS of tomorrow

10 - Create a *Persona Profile* for Success!

This is the single most important ingredient in achieving your Desired Outcome. By aligning your *Persona* with the *profile* of the *"person who would be successful"*, you will have the *mindset* to achieve the RESULTS you're after!

The Measure of Success

How do you measure your success? We've all seen that question used over and over in conversations, articles and books! We all want to *measure* our success!

When someone is successful, then the outcome of their achievement will be *desired and planned*. The *true measure* of success rests squarely with the achiever. Success should therefore be measured on an individual basis. Even though success cannot be measured by any conventional standard, you are encouraged to apply your individual measurements. When you create a new *Persona*, you want success to be measured based on your unique circumstances.

Success cannot be measured in any conventional and quantifiable way, but that does not diminish the *value of success*.

When it comes to success, you want to model the *profile* of the *"person who would be successful"*. It really doesn't matter that success is subjective. You need the emotional gratification that your INFLUENCERS *perceive* you as being successful. And occasionally you must pay a steep price for this perception. You may have to drive an expensive automobile, live in high-mortgaged house and exist on an ever-increasing line of credit.

Yet we all know that this measure of success is fraudulent.

This *perception* of success is artificially acquired and manipulated. And now it becomes a *deception*. In fact, the *illusion* of success is created by infusing tangible assets, such as an expensive automobile, a new house, a European vacation, etc. The *illusion* of social status is being substituted for success at the expense of values and virtues.

Lasting success cannot be achieved through deception or fraud. If your *perceived identity* and definition of success hinges on the acquisition of expensive toys and living a lavish lifestyles, you are not achieving success.

You are courting disaster!

The Value of Success

The value of a man should be seen in what he gives and not in what he is able to receive.
Try not to become a man of success,
but rather try to become a man of value.

~ Albert Einstein

When you try to determine the value of success, you must first acknowledge that success in itself is meaningless unless there is *value* attached to it. Success is not success, unless it has value and that value is a measure of what success brings and not takes away. You are not successful if you are the sole beneficiary of your success.

Success has no lasting value, unless the benefit of success is greater than success itself.

The value of success is measured by those who directly benefit from it. The value of this book is not measured by the number of copies it sells, but by the number of lives it impacts! It is not measured by how long it remains a best seller, but by its ability to change the *perception of "Who You Are"!*

The RESULTS that you will achieve, will be determined by your new *Persona* and how it impacts your INFLUENCERS; your family and friends, your loved ones, your associates, your business partners and everyone else who is part of your sphere of influence.

The value of your overall success will be determined by the benefits you bring to those who are impacted by you. Your legacy is therefore not determined by the number of your achievements, but by the benefits they bring!

♦　♦　♦　♦　♦

Signposts:

1. What are some of the values that your new *Persona* shares with the *"person who would be successful"*?

_____
_____
_____
_____
_____

2. Describe in your own words how you see the true value of success?

_____

_____

_____

_____

_____

3. What would make you feel successful and how would you express or display your success?

_____

_____

_____

_____

_____

4. How would you measure your achievements at a *personal* level, instead of measuring it against the criteria for success as prescribed by our social standards?

_____

_____

_____

_____

_____

5. Describe in your own words how the *seduction* of success can lead to the acquisition of expensive "toys" and a lavish lifestyle that is a fraudulent misrepresentation of success?

_____

_____

_____

_____

_____

MODULE VIII

Changing the Conversation!

Outline

- Your new *Persona* must be an effective communicator. When it speaks, it must be understood and not just heard! It must not only articulate your position with extreme clarity, it must also be able to defend it in debate! Voice intonations interpret your emotions, while at times silence is your best and most powerful ally and spokesperson.
- Your body language validates what your new *Persona* communicates and your spoken language articulates.
- Faith is the hardest thing to find and the easiest thing to lose! When things go wrong and we have no one left to blame, we blame ourselves and in doing so, we blame our faith and our belief!
- You can never go back to your past! Whatever happened in the Past is now irrelevant.

Every type of human interaction can be reduced to a single common denominator: COMMUNICATION!

The human voice can hypnotize or agonize. It can motivate or denigrate. It can command an army or whisper in a lover's ear. It can shatter crystal or sooth a crying child. It can carry the emotions of anger, love and joy. It can express jubilation or despair.

Your voice is a powerful communicator that can *instantaneously* change any existing *perceived identity* or create a new one! In order for you to achieve any Desired Outcome, you must first learn how to *control* and *command* your conversation!

There are four areas of *speech delivery* that are essential elements of verbal communication:

1 - The Power of Articulation

You must articulate your purpose and intent in a manner that leaves no room for misinterpretation. If your verbal communication is ambiguous, you will be *perceived* as "wishy washy". You may not always be able to control the way in which you are defined and characterized, but you should never leave the impressions you create to chance! You should always think before you speak and only speak after you've clearly formulated what you're going to say and how you're going to say it. Avoid any ambiguity and articulate any thoughts and messages in a clear and concise manner!

2 - The Power of Debate

Debating an issue is not the same as having a civilized argument. Debating is not about winning somebody over to your point of view, even though that may be the end result. A skilled debater is capable of articulating his or her view point in a powerful yet unintimidating fashion. Winning should never be the object of any debate, but a successfully debated issue will often result in one party acknowledging the superiority of the other party's point of view. And for you, that would be a highly civilized victory!

Never allow yourself to be drawn into an argument, but pick up the gauntlet when challenged to a debate over an issue you feel passionate about. Articulate your passion in a powerful and purposeful way! Regardless of the outcome, you will earn the respect and admiration of your challenger and will be defined and characterized accordingly!

3 - The Power of Voice Intonation

It isn't just what you say. It isn't just how well you articulate. It is the tone of your voice that speaks volumes! Speech and articulation reach us at an intellectual level. Intonation reaches us at an emotional level. Emotions are the most powerful motivators known to man.

Voice intonation is a double-edged sword however. It can instill trust and confidence, but it can also expose a weakness. You must always communicate from a position of strength! If your new *Persona* is a true, genuine, authentic and accurate representation of the *"person who would be successful"*, then you will be able to communicate from a position of strength! And you can use the power of voice intonation to leverage that strength!

4 - The Power of Silence

Silence can be deafening!

There are only two reasons for a person to be silent during a conversation:

1. A person has nothing to say, in which case there really is no conversation going on, *or*

2. The person has something to say, *but is not saying it!*

We all have experienced these moments of "awkward silence". It often happens when there is disagreement on an issue and the silent party stops articulating its point of view. And when that happens, the other person starts to panic. Nature abhors a vacuum, so we feel compelled to fill it!

We start to speak!

When we speak to break the silence, we are filling a void. And we fill that void *not* with well thought-out, meaningful and properly articulated dialogue. No, when we panic to fill the silence, we usually fill it with drivel!

Why do we feel so awkward during an extended period of silence? Why do we feel so compelled to fill the void? Why do we blink first?

Simple!

It is the *'fear of the unknown'*! We don't know what is on the other person's mind, if he/she doesn't speak it! That uncertainty is often intimidating and unnerving. And when silence is combined with body language, it can be downright scary! The proverbial calm before the storm!

If it is your client who breaks the silence, he/she is often at a disadvantage. Great salespeople have honed the technique of silence to a fine art. *Silence is control!*

You need to be in control of the conversation, in order to positively influence the way in which it is *perceived*. You must become an effective communicator. When you speak, you must be understood and not just heard!

You will occasionally be challenged on the positions you take. You must not only articulate your position with extreme clarity, you must also be able to defend it. You must be able to debate any position you take with passion and tenacity. And while you may not always win the debate, *you will always win respect!*

The nuances in your voice are the *interpreters* of your emotions. The intonations in your voice interpret your emotions. They convey your anger or displeasure. They betray your insincerities. They deliver feelings of love and affection. If the eyes are the windows to the soul, the voice is its echo chamber. The interpretation of your message will in large part depend on the intonation in your voice.

There will be times when silence is your best spokesperson. Let silence be an ally and not a distraction!

Of all the things that could be said, the words that aren't spoken are often the most powerful! They will always be understood, *but they will never come back to haunt you!*

The Pen is Mightier than the Sword!

You must create an accurate representation of your new *Persona* in both the spoken and written word. In other words, your written communications cannot be *perceived* as being less authentic than your spoken word. Your written word will become a permanent record of your spoken word and must accurately reflect what you intend to say!

This is particularly true for emails and social media posts. Poorly written messages can undermine your ability to be *perceived* as the *"person who would be successful"*. A hastily or sloppily composed email or an absurdly abbreviated text or 'tweet' can negatively impact the way you are perceived. Don't rely on poorly constructed emails and tweets to be the communicator of choice for your new *Persona*. When it comes to creating a lasting and positive impression, you must write carefully crafted and properly worded letters that are precise, to-the-point but above all, respectful of your target audience. Taking the extra time and care in preparing emails will go a long way to building the right *Persona*.

I recommended that you write at least one Personal Note per day to anyone in your sphere of influence; your family, friends, colleagues or anyone else who is an INFLUENCER. If you do this faithfully and consistently, you will build a very intimate level of trust and authority!

When was the last time that you received a personal note in the mail? Aside from seasonal wishes and birthdays, I bet that you probably can't remember the last spontaneous card that contained a personal and handwritten message!

Take a look at the messages you sent over the last week. Are there any repeat recipients? Are there any messages that have gone back and forth several times with each response getting shorter and more informal? Maybe you are simply communicating in a more efficient manner, with speed and to the (bullet) point! But that is not the way you should communicate with potential clients! Wearing blue jeans and t-shirts may be more comfortable but once in a while we all need to 'dress to impress'! So if you are sending out a bunch of emails that lack punctuation or capital letters and resemble the creative writings of a five year old, it's time to re-evaluate your communications strategies.

The Power of Body Language

> *Our speech delivers the message.*
> *Our body language validates it*
>
> ~Allan N. Mulholland

We create a *perception* about someone in the moment we see that person. We begin this *perception* when we meet or greet. We will expand on this *perception* when we make further contact with that person, but our initial *perception* is based on what we see in the moment and is created at the moment we see him or her.

Of course, the reverse holds true as well. Someone will create an initial *perception* about us, the moment they see us!

There are basically two ways in which we create initial *perceptions*. The first method is based on a crude profiling template, known as 'stereotyping'. We all have certain biases in favor or against a certain persona type and these biases are typically the result of social or cultural influences. They may also reflect our personal experiences with certain types of individuals. As we expand our profile of a person, these biases may give way to a more comprehensive profile that will either correct our initial bias or endorse it, giving further validity to our 'stereotype' model.

The second method is based on body language and creates a *perception* about a person based on their mannerisms, deportment and demeanor. It is in this area where you must put your best foot forward. It is really important that you adopt the body language of the *"person who would be successful"*.

What would be the deportment and demeanor of such a person?

Here are some of the more classic examples:

Sit or stand up straight	attentive
Shoulders up	tense
Shoulders down	relaxed
Arms crossed	defensive
Arms open	inviting
Legs crossed	protective
Legs uncrossed	casual
Hands fidgeting	nervous

Your new *Persona* is based on the *profile* of the *"person who would be successful"*! Your new *Persona* is therefore the "Social MASK" that represents the *"public perception"* of that person.

Your body language is the *"physical manifestation"* of your new *Persona*. On stage, an actor plays out his role by adapting his body language to the character he is playing!

You must adapt your body language to the character your new *Persona* is portraying!

The eyes are the windows to the soul

Are your eyes locked on a person when you meet and greet that someone? While there may be instances where culture or ceremony makes overt eye contact inappropriate, you have nothing to hide and your eyes should attest to that! You must look a person straight in the eye when you speak to them. Not only will it bolster your unspoken claim to authority, it will also reveal something about the person you're dealing with. Are their eyes meeting your gaze or are they searching for an escape? Does their focus on you support their stated intentions or are they wavering in their sincerity? Do they open the window to the soul or do they close the shutters?

Stand up and be counted

If your new *Persona* stands for something, your body language should speak up for it. Body language is often what makes a first impression, so let it make an impact!

The Purpose of Persuasion

Your *perceived identity* will be defined and characterized by those who are exposed to your new *Persona*. Your INFLUENCERS! Your new *Persona* will be developed from a comprehensive set of emotions, behaviors, sociological and linguistic patterns, as well as environmental influences and psychological and physiological characteristics. It will also incorporate your inherent personality traits which will give your new *Persona* its unique character!

Since your new *Persona* is inimitable, it will have both supporters and detractors. That is a fact that will never change. The purpose of persuasion is to change the ratio of supporters to detractors heavily in your favor. To achieve the Desired Outcome you are looking for, you will need support from relatives and friends, co-workers and bosses, teachers and other leaders.

"No man is an island!"

Thirst for Knowledge

Your new *Persona* comes with a certificate of authenticity, but (unfortunately) not with a college diploma or university degree. If you were fortunate enough to attend Kindergarten, you probably learned most of what you need to know in life! But you must constantly update and upgrade your knowledge base. No, you don't have to go back to school. You're already attending the University of Life. But knowledge is power and the more you know, the more powerful and effective will be your new *Persona*.

Always thirst for knowledge. I have never met a person who suffered from too much knowledge. Your new *Persona* derives its power from knowledge. Feed it frequently! It's always hungry for more and has an insatiable appetite for *quality content*.

But keep your thirst for knowledge focused on the results. What does your new *Persona* need to do to achieve those results? What knowledge is functional and what is frivolous to creating your Desired Outcome? Will your acquired knowledge keep you on top of your game or will it bog you down? Select your knowledge base carefully and prudently and then collect as much knowledge as is needed to achieve your Desired Outcome.

What type of knowledge should you acquire? That of course depends on the results you want to achieve!

For example, if you are looking to find a new relationship, your knowledge base should contain as much information as possible about the interests, hobbies, activities, likes and dislikes of your potential romantic interest.

If you want to land that dream job or are pursuing a new career, you must come prepared with compelling résumé and a mental dossier loaded with facts and figures about your future employer.

If you want to start your own business, don't rely on just a franchisee manual and a blueprint for making perfect French fries. You must be knowledgeable about your new industry, your competitors and current market trends. You should also do a financial evaluation of your new business from the day you open the doors to the public, because that is also the day that your business is officially 'For Sale'!

If you want to beat a drug or alcohol addiction, you need to research proven techniques and technologies to deal with the addiction. Select the cure that will work best with your new *Persona* and then make that cure your new addiction!

If you want to lose excess weight, rely on knowledge and not on hype. *Common sense* is the best weight loss program I know of personally! Let common sense guide you in your research and then opt for the program that best suits your new *Persona*. Putting less *in* the body to put less *on* the body seems to be a common sense approach!

If you want a deeper connection with your faith, you may want to expand your knowledge and understanding about your faith. Some religions preach the practice of having *blind faith*, but you probably prefer to see where your faith is taking you!

You should acquire knowledge in abundance and collect it whenever and wherever you can! It is your key to Personal Growth!

The Driving Force of Emotions

> *Emotions are internal fragmentations*
> *that form an external façade when released*
>
> ~Allan N. Mulholland

If knowledge is the power behind your new *Persona*, then emotions are its driving force!

There are four ways in which you will deal with negative or destructive emotions:

1. **Avoidance**

    You may have tried to avoid dealing with your emotions. In order to avoid rejection in the past, you may have tried to avoid any emotions that can ultimately lead to rejection. And that fear of rejection may have stopped you from entering into a new relationship. As a result, you avoided the experience of feeling love, intimacy and connection. Your new *Persona* must not try to avoid negative emotions and experiences, but rather face them head on!

2. **Denial**

    You may have tried to deny any negative emotions or experiences. You may have tried to disassociate yourself from these feelings. But your new *Persona* will not deny the existence of negative emotions and experiences because eventually, they will erupt.

3. **Endurance**

    You may have tried to *endure* your negative emotions and experiences, allowing them to inflict psychological and emotional pain! Your new *Persona* will not use negative emotions as leverage. Instead, it will neutralize negative emotions by focusing on their positive counterparts.

4. Elimination

You may have tried to *harbor* your negative emotions and experiences, thereby perpetuate their destructive influence. But your new *Persona* will try to convert negative emotions into positive experiences and learn from past mistakes.

Your new *Persona* also manages the ways in which you experience other emotions, such as anger, overwhelm, depression, frustration and loneliness. With your new *Persona*, you will be able to change the ways in which you deal with these emotions. A new *Persona* can neutralize the negative consequences of these emotions and experiences. Every emotion carries a message that you must interpret and convert into some type of re-action! First, you must analyze the emotion and identify what it represents. If the emotion is negative, you must try and neutralize it or convert it into a positive emotion. Next, you must change the way you communicate this feeling.

The most important thing to remember about emotions:
a) The power of an emotion is in the significance you attach to that emotion!
b) No emotion, negative or positive, will have any lasting influence unless you give significance to that emotion!
c) If the emotion is in conflict with your new *Persona*, you must change the significance until the emotion produces a positive outcome.

Here is a list of some of the most common emotions that you will experience on a regular basis:

Positive Feelings & Emotions		Negative Feelings & Emotions	
joy	love	frustration	Insecurity
success	flexibility	sadness	boredom
contribution	impactful	impatient	anger
creativity	power	anxious	annoyed
curiosity	beauty	guilt	unsure
wonder	spirituality	disrespect	depression
respect	kindness	loneliness	humiliation
sincerity	integrity		

Teach!

Your new *Persona* is a highly qualified teacher. It represents your life's experience in a unique and unorthodox way by being the *Persona* for your Future and not from your Past. Yet it is also the product of your collective history that is encapsulated in your 'Equity of the Past', without the burden of all the baggage you acquired over the years.

Start Communicating With Your Faith!

Faith is the hardest thing to find and the easiest thing to lose!

~Allan N. Mulholland

There are many ways for you to express your affiliation with your faith. You can attend church as part of a congregation or you can worship in the privacy of your inner spiritual world. Whatever your choice of belief and type of worship, the ability to believe is one of the most powerful motivating forces known to mankind.

Your faith should be a very private and personal choice. If your faith is part of your core values, your new *Persona* will enshrine that faith with respect and deference.

Stop Communicating With the Past!

"Why did this happen to me?"

Have you ever found yourself in a situation where that seemed an appropriate question? We usually ask ourselves this question when something bad befalls us. When tragedy strikes or when misfortune detours our life. Yet many psychologists and counselors consider this question inappropriate or not empowering. It is too vague and does not solicit a structured and specific answer!

Personally, I think it's one of the greatest questions you can ask, which is probably why so many people are asking this very question! If you believe that 'everything happens for a reason', then the question of *"why did this happen to me?"* is indeed a valid one! Esoterically, you already know that 'it happened for a reason'! The question simply acknowledges our human limitations in deducing what that reason was!

The more important question you may want to ask yourself is: *"Does it really matter that things happened for a reason?"* The answer is NO. Whatever may have happened for a reason *also happened in the Past! And whatever happened in the Past is now irrelevant.*

We can never go back to our Past!

But you can choose to retain your 'Equity of the Past' by making your most valuable experiences from the Past a part of your Future. Without a Past there can be no Future. And now you get to choose what you want to bring forward! Once you've selected your "Equity of the Past", you must let go of rest! Whatever decisions you make from this day forward will not in any way alter your past, so let it be!

♦ ♦ ♦ ♦ ♦

Signposts:

1. What are some of the communication skills that you need In order to tap into the power of the *spoken word*?

_____

_____

_____

_____

_____

2. What are some of the techniques you can use to enhance the power of the *written word*?

_____

_____

_____

_____

_____

3. How would you adapt your *body language* to validate your new *Persona?* How would you sit, stand and move?

_____

_____

_____

_____

_____

4. In what ways can you tap into the *power of knowledge*?

_____

_____

_____

_____

_____

5. Do you still think about the past and the missed opportunities, even though the past is irrelevant?

_____

_____

_____

_____

_____

MODULE IX

Code of Conduct

Outline

- Your new *Persona* must exude *confidence* in the performance of its role as the *"person who would be successful"*, or it will be judged as weak and inferior. A new *Persona* that conducts with confidence will be able to achieve anything that is an absolute MUST!
- Integrity is the moral compass of your new *Persona*.
- Determination will keep you on target. Purpose will keep you on course!
- Without *passion*, there can never be a complete sense of fulfillment. When you follow your dreams and stay true to your convictions, you will eventually discover your passion!

As you continue to build the foundation for your new *Persona*, it's time to create a Code of Conduct for the *"person who would be successful"*!

Confidence

If your new *Persona* does not exude *confidence* in the performance of its role as the *"person who would be successful"*, the performance will be judged as weak and inferior.

In a new relationship, a lack of confidence can be considered a weakness that can ultimately lead to a *perceived* imbalance in the roles each partner will play. If you are typecast to play a supporting role in the relationship, you may be in for an unhappy and rocky ride! If, on the other hand, you conducts yourself with an air of confidence, you will likely share equal billing in the relationship!

When considering a career move or applying for a new job, the confident way in which you conduct yourself is key to getting the job. If you show a level of confidence in your ability to be the *"person who would be the successful candidate"*, a new employer will interpret that confidence as a measure of conduct that will give you the edge over the other applicants.

Confidence in the market place is a strong determinant of stock value. Consumer confidence can build or destroy an economy! Corporations will not be able to attract lenders and investors without the underlying confidence that their business is sound and profitable.

Integrity

Your new *Persona* must be a true, genuine, authentic and accurate representation of the *"person who would be successful"*. If you compromise your integrity, your new *Persona* becomes a *disingenuous copy* of someone else!

Many life coaches, behavioral analysts and personal development experts preach the 'modeling' technique as a means of achieving success. They are of the naive and mistaken belief that achieving success is as simple as copying someone who already is successful! Virtually any self-improvement course is somehow based on this philosophy.

They'll all tell you: *"Just copy someone who already is successful and you will also be successful. Why re-invent the wheel?"*

WHY INDEED!

But here's the 'catch 22' question that invariably asks *"If being successful is that simple, why doesn't everybody just model someone who already is successful?"*

For you to be successful, you must be a true, genuine, authentic and accurate representation of the *"person who would be successful"* and not simply a *copy* of someone else! In other words, your new *Persona* should not only model the *"person who would be successful"*.

You must in fact becomes that person!

Integrity is the moral compass of your new *Persona*. Without integrity, your next relationship will be susceptible to disingenuous influences such as jealousy, distrust, apprehension and suspicion. Without integrity, your next career move will be just another lateral change. Without integrity, your business will not thrive. Without integrity, you will not be able to face the demons of your

addictions. Without integrity, you will not stick to a
healthy and balanced diet or a new fitness regime.

Without integrity you will not develop a deeper
connection with your faith.

Your new *Persona* must operate from a place of integrity.
And even if the imperfections of your new *Persona* will
occasionally cause misalignments with your *perceived
identity*, your integrity must always remain beyond
reproach!

Purpose & Determination

Thomas Edison once said that *"Success is 10% inspiration
and 90% perspiration"*. I believe that ultimate success is
the result of 100% determination! Achievement at its
highest level must be matched by equivalent
determination.

It takes 100% determination to make something an
absolute MUST. Determination is the opportunity cost for
achieving success! If 'Determination' is your pilot then
'Purpose' is the co-pilot in the cockpit of your new
Persona. 'Purpose' navigates the plane! You must be
absolutely clear on your goals and objectives. You must
have a detailed flight plan.

With 'Determination' flying your plane and 'Purpose'
navigating your course, you need to check your fuel gauge.
The journey to success is never a direct flight and you will
have to make some detours. There will be turbulence
along the way and you will be flying through a severe

weather systems, guaranteed! Strong headwinds will slow you down and dense fog will throw you off your course!

But no matter what happens during the flight, 'Purpose' will keep the plane on target. 'Determination' will do the rest!

Have a safe flight!

Passion

I am absolutely passionate about life & business coaching!

I never fully understood why I felt so passionate about coaching until I read Anthony Robbins *"Awakening the Giant Within"*. One of the key components of Mr. Robbins' remarkable insight into the human psyche is his masterful analysis of the 'Six Human Needs'. He concluded that every human being, regardless of race, beliefs, background or experience has these Six Human Needs that determine the quality of their lives. They are:

1. certainty
2. uncertainty/variety
3. significance
4. love/connection
5. growth
6. contribution

If you're not familiar with Anthony Robbins, I highly recommend that you read his books or purchase his audio or video programs. They set the standard for modern behavioral psychology.

My passion for coaching fulfills each one of these Six Human Needs.

1.   I find *certainty* in the knowledge that I create permanent change for my clients by altering their *Persona*.

2.   I find *uncertainty/variety* in the many challenges my clients face and need solutions for!

3.   I find *significance* in being able to help my clients achieve their Desired Outcome.

4.   I find the feelings of *love and connection* through my relationship with my clients.

5.   I achieve personal and spiritual *growth* through my connection with my clients.

6.   I *contribute* by facilitating my clients in achieving their goals.

I am truly blessed, humbled and grateful for the life, purpose and mission God bestowed upon me. But of all the triggers that make me an achiever, such as my dogged determination, my unwavering focus on my goal and my tenacity to succeed, it truly is my passion that makes me feel fulfilled!

You may have all the necessary qualities to achieve success. But until you discover your true passion, there will never be a complete sense of fulfillment.

Passion is unique to each individual. There is no formula for creating passion. It is simply there, waiting to be discovered! Love is our strongest emotion. Passion is our deepest conviction. If you follow your dreams and stay true to your convictions, you will eventually discover your true passion.

♦   ♦   ♦   ♦   ♦

Signposts:

1. Identify a goal or objective that you can achieve over the next two weeks! Will achieving this goal bolster your self-confidence? Will it benefit others?

_____

_____

_____

_____

2. Now list 10 things you are determined to do to reach your goal or objective. What are you prepared to give up? What skills are you prepared to acquire? What knowledge are you prepared to gain? What sacrifices are you prepared to make? What lifestyle changes are you prepared to implement?

_____

_____

_____

_____

_____

_____

_____

_____

3. How will you align your integrity with the results you want to achieve? How would you protect your integrity from being compromised?

_____

_____

_____

_____

4. What are you truly passionate about? How long have you felt this passion? Why do you feel so passionate?

_____

_____

_____

_____

5. Describe in your own words your idea of a daily health & fitness regime. Which healthy habits will you adopt? Which habits will you eliminate? Will you work out on a regular basis?

_____

_____

_____

_____

6. How would you describe the core values of your faith?

_____

_____

_____

_____

_____

♦ ♦ ♦ ♦ ♦

MODULE X

Plugging Into Your INFLUENCERS

Outline

- You will connect the dots between your new *Persona* and the people who are your INFLUENCERS. They may include a spouse or partner, children, relatives, friends, co-workers, employers and members of your community!
- Relatives can be an enormous source of support for you. But they can also be an exasperating irritant in your quest for a new beginning.
- Friends come into your life for a reason, a season or a lifetime!
- Your new *Persona* must be that of a community leader.

Objective

Your new *Persona* is now a partially developed picture that needs to be completed by connecting the dots that link the various relationships you have with your INFLUENCERS.

Connecting the Dots

One of my favorite pastimes as a child was to open up a puzzle book and flip to the page that showed what appeared to be a collection of randomly strewn dots over a partly drawn picture, with each dot having an assigned number adjacent to it. Connect the dots in their numerical sequence 'et voilà', the full picture emerges!

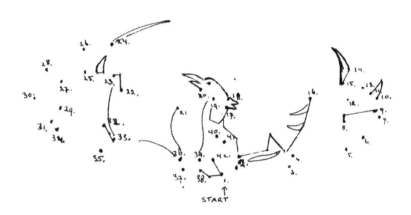

Each one of these dots represents a connection between you and a person who is a significant player in your life, moving forward. In other words, an INFLUENCER! They do not include people from the past with whom you have no further association or are not a part of your 'Equity of the Past'!

Spouse, Partner or 'Significant Other'

For most people, their most important relationship is with their spouse, partner or 'significant other'.
I'm quick to make a distinction here! While the relationship with a partner may be the most important from a *pragmatic* perspective, the bond between a parent and a child is often stronger at an *emotional* level!

What *is* relevant however, is your new *Persona*. If your relationship is new and still in the early stages of development, what will be the qualities and character traits of the *"person who would be successful"* in making the relationship work? In order for the relationship to work, you want to develop a *Persona* that is aligned with the *profile* of your partner.

In other words, what are the essential elements of your new *Persona* that must also be present in your spouse or partner's *persona profile*?

- What qualities would be advanced by the merger of these two profiles?
- Which interests are common to both *profiles?*
- Which anomalies must be addressed?
- Are the objectives of the partners of mutual benefit and in consort with one another?
- Are they socially and culturally compatible?
- Are the INFLUENCERS on both sides compatible?

Developing a *Persona* that is congruent with the *profile* of a partner, is an essential first step in achieving the RESULTS your client is looking for!

Children

Raising children is a challenge at the best of times!

Raising children in this day and age can be very stressful and, at times, overwhelming. As parents, we are often out-of-touch with all the new developments and social pressures that influence our children. Our society, with a little help from some savvy marketers and retailers, has created a sub-culture in which our kids can find commonality.

There is no doubt that the demands on raising our children are often in conflict with the reality of our hectic lifestyles. We work harder to produce more while delivering less. It is the conundrum of the age of technology! But while our children may be more susceptible to unwanted and often undesirable external influences, they are still children and it is our duty as parents and society as a whole to provide them with the best upbringing possible.

Our role as parents is to guide our children through their developmental stages. But each child is unique. Each child is an individual. Each child has its own identity. There is no mold that fits all!

A child's *Persona* is a reflection of its primary INFLUENCERS. If you are *disconnected* from your children, then now is the time to change. Your new *Persona* will be that of the *"person who would be"* a parent and a role model. This new *Persona* must re-establish your connection with your children, whether they are four or forty! You must mend broken dreams and fences. You reassert your presence and lead your children with a vision for their future.

Relatives

Do you sometimes wish that you could have chosen your relatives the way you choose your friends or relationships? Unfortunately, when you enter into a new relationship with a partner, their relatives are the 'baggage that comes with the package'!

Relatives can be an enormous source of support for you. But they can also be an exasperating irritant in your quest for a new beginning. They may have well-meant advice to impart or solutions to offer, but often times their counsel is best ignored! As INFLUENCERS they should be respected. Just make sure that their influence is of a limited capacity!

Friends

True friends are your greatest source of support. True friends don't judge or condemn. They simply accept, often enthusiastically. As long as you remain true to your *identity*, true friends will believe in you! Because that's what true friends are for!

True friends are measured by their quality. You may have dozens of 'acquaintances', but in times of crisis you soon discover who your true friends are! True friends earned the right to be part of your *inner circle*. You must re-evaluate the connections they have with all of their friends.

Someone said that *"People come into your life for a reason, a season or a lifetime"*. I believe that to be especially true for friends. If they come into your life for a reason, they will often complete their assigned mission and then leave again when the task is completed. If they come into your life for a season, they are usually a part of your journey and will likely disappear once you've reached a certain destination.

True friends often stay for a lifetime!

Employer

The influence an employer has on you is usually of an economic nature. Sure, they may be friends or in some other way have an impact, but the most direct influence is delivered in the form of a paycheck.

Yet the relationship between employer and employee is often strained. There is a new disease that is of such epidemic proportions that it has infected almost six out of every ten Americans currently in the work force. It is the silent killer of ambition, innovation, creativity and productivity. It is the antithesis of the American Dream. And it is affecting a way of life for millions of people.

The disease is called *job dissatisfaction* and it is spreading like a wildfire throughout our nation, in every industry and every job sector. This malaise affects the physical, emotional and spiritual health of those afflicted. It is a cancer on the average income earner.

No age or income group is immune to this disease. In fact, employees under the age of 25 express the highest level of dissatisfaction ever recorded by surveys for that age group. Job dissatisfaction spells serious trouble for the overall engagement of U.S. employees and ultimately for employee productivity. All this at a time when our Gross Domestic Product (GDP) is under constant pressure from oversees labor pools.

One of the great benefits of creating a new *Persona* is that it can reverse this trend by changing the *perception* of the job, as well as the *perception* of employer.

For the first stage of this transformation, your *perception* of your job must be aligned with your *perception* of the contribution the job makes to the community or society at large. Making a contribution and creating a benefit is a powerful emotional stimulus that often exceeds the financial benefit of having a job. This is a factor that is often overlooked by short-sighted employers who can only express the value of their business in economic terms. They totally ignore the value of their human capital!

The second stage of this transformation occurs when you try to align your job with your True Identity. Much of job dissatisfaction stems from the misalignment of your *True Identity* and the profile of the *"person who would be successful"* in the performance of the job. Sometimes this *misalignment* is severe and you will not be able to perform the functions of your job because it compromises your *value system* or violates some core belief. If that is the case, you will never find a level of satisfaction to perform the required functions of the job and you're better off finding new and different employment.

But many times the *profile* of the *"person who would be successful"* in the performance of the job can be aligned with your new *Persona* when they are "merged".

Aligning these two profiles to the point where they complement each other in a positive and productive fashion creates a unique synergy between the job and the person performing it!

Business

Here's a question that many small business owners face on a continual basis:

"Should they work <u>on</u> their business, or <u>in</u> their business?"

The answer is often vague and confusing. Most business owners do both. In his book *"The E-Myth Revisited"*, Michael Gerber describes the typical small business owner as wearing three hats and often all three at the same time.

In his now famous analogy, he depicts the three personas of the business owner as the *'Entrepreneur'*, the *'Manager'* and the *'Technician'*. The *'Entrepreneur'* conceptualizes the business, the *'Manager'* operates the business and the *'Technician'* produces the product. If it hadn't been for Sarah's Pie Shop 'model', we'd still be wondering which hat to wear and when!

There are two distinct but equally important levels of connectivity that the *Persona* of a business owner must bring to his shop.

First, there is the connection with the staff and employees. Your new *Persona* must clearly define your role as the owner/manager of your business enterprise. The success or failure of the business ultimately rests with you. A recession may affect the market that your business serves. A competitor may drive down your price point. The industry that your supply to may go under.

Secondly, there is the connection with your customers. You must create the right *Persona* to deliver your message of consumer service, customer care and client appreciation.

And make sure that your new *Persona* wears three hats!

Community

Your community is the micro-society in which you live and work. Your community is the place where you raise your family and where you visit your friends and neighbors. You attend your place of worship in your community. Your children attend school there. It's where they play baseball in the summer and hockey in the winter. You give to your community in terms of your involvement and the community gives back by providing a safe and secure place for you to live.

Your community must also be able to create an environment for your new *Persona* to grow and prosper. It must be the right community for the *"person who would be successful"*!

Your community is home to the *"Leader within"*. The *"Leader within"* takes pride in his/her community and safeguards it against potential harm. The *"Leader within"* protects the children and the elderly that live within its boundaries. "Soccer moms" are leaders when they organize carpooling to the local Saturday game. Church leaders participate in the Sunday picnic after service. Business leader sponsor fundraisers for local volunteer organizations.

Your community is dependent on its leaders and the leaders depend on their community. Your new *Persona* must be that of a community leader. When your new *Persona* is in harmony with the community, both will grow and prosper!

Goals & Objectives

Next, we will focus on connecting you with your goals and objectives. If you're still not totally clear on your goals and objectives, there are hundreds of books and programs that will show you how to set your goals. All these programs work to some extent! They all use "Goal Setting Tools" and lay out a timeline on achievement. Some have workbooks and online calendars that automatically notify you when you must take your next *action step*. Some even have a goal tracker that measures progress!

Your goals and objectives are projected onto the future and it is important to connect your new *Persona* with these goals and objectives, so you will have a clear understanding about the direction you must take!

Signposts:

1. Who are your main INFLUENCERS?

_____

_____

_____

_____

_____

2. Why are these INFLUENCERS significant?

_____

_____

_____

_____

_____

3. Are there any areas of your life that you want to make significant changes to?

_____

_____

_____

_____

_____

4. What is your message to your children? "Nothing ventured, nothing gained!" or "Better safe than sorry"? Why did you choose this option?

_____

_____

_____

_____

_____

5. Can you name 3 true friends who will support your new *Persona?*

_____

_____

_____

_____

6. Do you love your current job or would you rather *shove it?* Would your relationship with your employer be different, if you approached it as a leader instead of a follower?

_____

_____

_____

_____

7. How can you become more active in your community?

_____

_____

_____

_____

8. What are the top three results you want to achieve over the next 3 – 6 months? You are developing a new *Persona* to achieve these goals, so make sure that each one of them is an absolute MUST!

_____

_____

_____

_____

_____

_____

MODULE XI
Creating RESULTS!

Outline

- In order for you to succeed at achieving your 'MUST goals and objectives', you must become the *"person who would be successful"*. That person is the *"Definitive Leader"*!
- You will seek out *"Resolute Relationships"* that are eminently of benefit to you, to others and ultimately make a contribution to the Greater Good.
- You must become an *"Intrepid Entrepreneur"*. You will not listen to the voices of doom and gloom. You are intolerant of self-doubt! You are fearless in the face of adversity!
- Enduring friendships exist as long as the profile created *for* you is matched by the profile created *by* you!

Your new *Persona* is nearing completion. Soon it will be ready to assume the role of the *"Definitive Leader"*, create *"Resolute Relationships"*, become an *"Intrepid Entrepreneur"*, build *"Enduring Friendships"* and experience *"Lasting Love"*.

Definitive Leadership

Definitive Leadership originates from within and then transcends all barriers and boundaries of physical limitations.

Where the follower says *"I cannot do this"*, the leader asks *"How can I do this"?* A child learns how to walk, because it MUST! A prisoner of war survives his internment, because he MUST! A mother protects her children, because she MUST!

As Definitive Leaders, you will maintain your faith, hold on to your values and stay true to your principles - *because you MUST!*

No matter the odds, if it is a MUST, you will achieve your Desired Outcome! But first you must become *a "Definitive Leader"*!

We all have inherent leadership qualities but not all leadership is equally developed! The standard convention by which our society defines leadership makes it virtually impossible for the majority to achieve leadership status.

Definitive Leaders takes charge and are in control of their lives! The *Definitive Leader* does not shirk his responsibilities! Never! Not to his family and friends. Not to his country. Not to his peers. Not to his work. Not to his faith and his convictions. Never!

The *Definitive Leader* does not abdicate his role as leader. Ever! Not as a parent. Not as a caregiver. Not as a citizen. Not as a worker.

"This is not my job!" is the excuse of a follower!

"This is my responsibility!" is the creed of the *Definitive Leader.*

The *Definitive Leader* leads by example. Always! She is a role model for her children. She is an inspiration to her co-workers. She is a hands-on leader who will do 'whatever it takes'. She does not shy away from menial tasks for she understands that everything in the Universe has purpose and in some way contributes to the Greater Good.

The *Definitive Leader* always has a reason for doing things and never an excuse for neglecting anything. Ever! She is an active participant in her community. She picks up the slack when someone lags behind. She is focused on the task at hand. She has a vision for the future. She takes charge whenever there is a void. She takes control whenever there is a vacuum.

The *Definitive Leader* is committed to his purpose and he lives by his commitments. Always! His word is his bond and his actions always validate his word. He is committed to his family. His is committed as a provider and a protector. He is committed to his work or business. He is committed to achieving his personal goals and the goals which are entrusted to him by his employer. And he is committed to his faith.

The *Definitive Leader* is disciplined and follows through. Always! He has an internal taskmaster to keep him on track and on time. His vision is also his compass. He is beholden to no one, but respectful of all!

Whatever purpose, goal or objective your new *Persona* is entrusted with, 'IT' will achieve success by becoming the *"person who would be successful"*. Once you are perceived, defined and characterized as a *Definitive Leader*, you will have become that person!

Resolute Relationships

"No man is an island!"

You will look for support groups within your community. You will reach out to those who can advance your cause and who will benefit from your achievements.

You will seek guidance and advice from those who have a genuine and altruistic desire to help. You will seek counsel from those who are in a position to impart counsel. With your new *Persona*, you will be able to create meaningful and powerful relationships.

Resolute Relationships!

As human beings, we all seek a connection. It is part of our social makeup. Even those who proclaim to be loners and lead a reclusive lifestyle rely on society to safeguard their ascetic existence. True relationships are built on trust and respect. They have reciprocity of value. They provide a safe harbor for those who seek emotional shelter. They provide comfort to those in need. They give direction to those who are lost. They give hope, when hope is gone!

Resolute Relationships are true relationships!

At the core of any relationship is the strength of our ties to those with whom we seek a connection. For most of us that is our immediate family. There is no greater source for love and connection than the one emanating from our own family. Our family values are a sacred trust. They must be upheld and protected. Especially against those who claim to have "moral superiority" and tend to judge family values by their own self-righteous narrow-mindedness.

Your new *Persona* will consider family as the #1 Resolute Relationship!

Your true friends are the next level of connection to which you will feel a strong affinity. More than any other relationship, true friends will be neutral and non-judgmental in their acceptance of you. They may be reluctant at first to embrace your new *Persona*, but they will be prepared to accept you regardless of their trepidations.

Your second Resolute Relationship is therefore with your true friends!

Other Resolute Relationships can be forged and fostered with co-workers, board members, country club buddies and members of a professional association. You can have Resolute Relations with fellow worshippers. You can have Resolute Relationships at work or at play.
You must seek out the Resolute Relationships that are eminently of benefit to them, to others and ultimately make a contribution to the Greater Good.

Resolute Relationships strengthen the fabric of society and bolster the resilience of your new *Persona*!

The Intrepid Entrepreneur

Are you self-employed?

As more and more people are looking for work because the company they were employed by is no longer in business or the industry of which they were once a proud participant is no longer viable in today's economy, the ranks of the self-employed have proliferated at exponential increments.

The dream of entrepreneurship was once the exclusive domain of a rare breed of visionaries and risk takers. But today's economic realities have brought the notion of free enterprise back to Main Street, where self-employment is often the only viable alternative to unemployment.

And from the ashes of a devastated economy rises a new free-enterprise model: *"The Intrepid Entrepreneur"*! Perhaps it would be more apt to describe this new breed of "self-employed unemployed" as *reluctant* entrepreneurs.

After all, they were forced out of their comfort zone and tossed into the unfamiliar world of free-enterprise where *'survival of the fittest'* is the mantra of the day!

Many a reluctant entrepreneur has also become the victim of a new type of predator; the infomercial promoters and online marketing gurus! These 'snake oil' salesmen have the 'secret' to entrepreneurial wealth and it's yours to have for three equal payments of $79.95. Risk free and with all the templates needed to make you an instant money machine! No experience required! After all, the guru who is preaching this stuff was broke and on the street less than two years ago, but now lives in a villa overlooking South Point Beach! And now you too can live the American dream, as long as you have a valid credit card with room to spare!

Your new *Persona* will be anything but reluctant! If fact, it should be downright tenacious! 'IT' will not listen to the voices of doom and gloom. 'IT' is intolerant of self-doubt! 'IT' is fearless in the face of adversity.

Your new *Persona* is an *intrepid entrepreneur*!

Enduring Friendships

With your new *Persona* in place, you will choose new friends and lose some old friends in the process. It's all a part of your evolutionary path to a Desired Outcome! Friends will come into your life for a reason, a season or a lifetime.

But friendships are never *unconditional*! We create a *perceived identity* for every human being we ever come into contact with, based on our *perception* of that person. The more we care about another person, the more detailed will be our *perception* of that person. Our friendship for a person is strengthened as long as our *perception* of that person matches or exceeds the friendship we created.

A *perceived identity* is always fluid and will change over time. We usually adjust the *perception* we create about someone to match any changes they make to their *Persona*. The closer we are to a person, the more apt we become at aligning their *Persona* with the *perceptions* we created about them.

But there may come a time when the *image* we created about a person can no longer be stretched any further! If the image we created gets stretched too far, the image will become distorted, warped or fragmented!

And that's when friendship will become conditional!

Enduring friendships exist as long as the profile created *for* us is matched by the profile created by us! ! When that happens, you will enjoy an enduring friendship.

Lasting Love

Lasting love may be the epiphany of romantic poets, but for many people the concept of lasting love is a failed experiment from the past. As cynical as that may sound, it is the harsh reality for many unsuccessful relationships and indicative of our staggering divorce rate. Any amelioration of these statistics is simply an exercise in 'living in denial'.

If failure is the greatest pain known to man, then 'failed love' is a double whammy! If you were once truly in love and all of a sudden found yourself 'suddenly single' through circumstances beyond your control, you'll know what that pain feels like! Is it any wonder that so many 'suddenly singles' are choosing a life without a partner, rather than risking the possibility of future abandonment?

In order to create lasting love, we must understand the dynamics of a relationship at its core. Love is the most powerful emotion known to man. Love can ignite at a moment's notice. A casual smile. A flirtatious wink. A passionate kiss.

Love can also develop over time. Lasting love often takes a long time to mature. When we first experience that burst of passion which usually accompanies 'falling in love', we create a profile for the subject of our attraction. If that profile is aligned with our own *Persona,* we have 'chemistry'! If, on the other hand, that profile is in conflict with our own *Persona*, we have the potential for disaster!

We can try to modify our *Persona Profile* to create a better match or we can arrogantly assume that we can change the person who has become our 'love interest'. Good luck on both fronts. Marriage counselors and divorce lawyers just love people who think that way!

For lasting love to occur, two fundamentals must be in play:
1. The profile of your love interest matches that of your own *Persona*. They must both qualify as the *"person who would be successful"* at creating lasting love.
2. Both *Personas* merge together for a lasting future. The power of lasting love is in the sum of two compatible *Personas*.

Signposts:

1. What are the characteristics of a *Definitive Leader*?

_____

_____

_____

_____

_____

2. What are the qualities of a Resolute Relationship?

_____

_____

_____

_____

_____

3. Name the characteristics of an *Intrepid Entrepreneur?*

_____

_____

_____

_____

_____

4. Create a descriptive profile for the *"person who would be successful"* in winning your heart. Do you know that person? Or are you still looking?

_____

_____

_____

_____

_____

MODULE XII
The Person Who Would Be Successful!

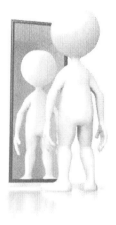

Over the past 12 Modules, you have created a *perceived identity* and a *Persona* that is based on the *profile* of the *"person who would be successful"!* Now it's time to create the *perception* that you desire and achieve your Desired Outcome! You've already created the *perception* of your Desired Outcome. All you need to do now is make this perception your personal *reality!* Let's close the "Cycle of Identity"!

It's time to congratulate you on achieving a major *milestone!* Your new *Persona* is complete and you are now ready to take on the *identity* of the *"person who would be successful"!* And with the completion of your new *Persona*, you have now become *"that person"!*

The personal and professional transformations that you experienced by implementing the 12 Modules will be amazing!

127

You have:

• Changed your *perceived identity* that was responsible for the situation you were in at the beginning of this program!

• Broken the "Cycle of Identity" and created the identity you desire!

• Re-visited the "Restore Point" from where you followed a different path to your Desired Outcome.

• Taken control over the way in which you are perceived by developing a new *Persona*. This new *Persona* contains the blueprint (profile) of the *"person who would be successful"*. This is the person you now have become!

• Learned how to measure your results by aligning them with your new *Persona*. Results that can't be measured can't be managed!

• Learned how to communicate your message to your INFLUENCERS.

• Developed a Code of Conduct for your new *Persona*.

• Established or renewed relationships with all your INFLUENCERS.

If you are looking to attract the right partner to build an ideal relationship with, you can align your new *Persona* with the *profile* of the *"person who would be successful"* in building such a relationship.

By aligning your new *Persona* with the 7 elements of the *profile* for the *"person who would be successful"*, you can:

- Assimilate the emotional patterns, such as:
    o Love
    o Affection
    o Respect
    o Trust

- Assimilate the behavioral patterns, such as:
  - Manners
  - Etiquette
  - Attire
  - Personal hygiene
- Assimilate the sociological patterns, such as:
  - Ability to interact
  - Being part of a community
  - Social values
  - Shared objectives
- Assimilate the linguistic patterns, such as:
  - Conversation
  - Communication
  - Using proper language skills
  - Self-expression
- Assimilate the environmental influences, such as:
  - Alkaline (positive) influences
  - Acidic (negative) influences
  - Toxic (destructive) influences
- Assimilate psychological characteristics, such as:
  - Control (Responsibility, self-esteem, etc.)
  - Influence (Trust, Respect, Motivation, etc.)
  - Contribution (Attitude, Accountability, etc.)
  - Growth (Vision, Personal Development, etc.)
- Assimilate physiological characteristics, such as:
  - Deportment
  - Energy
  - Lifestyle
  - Awareness

If you are looking to land that dream job or promotion, you can align your new *Persona* with the *profile* of the *"person who would be successful"* in career building.

By aligning your new *Persona* with the 7 elements of the *profile* for the *"person who would be successful"*, they can:

- Assimilate the emotional patterns, such as:
    - Sociable
    - Stable
    - Adaptable
    - Curiosity
- Assimilate the behavioral patterns, such as:
    - Performance
    - Attitude
    - Personality
    - Interpersonal relationships
- Assimilate the sociological patterns, such as:
    - Adapting corporate philosophy
    - Being part of a team
    - Corporate values
    - Company objectives
- Assimilate the linguistic patterns, such as:
    - Interview skills
    - Familiarity with job related nomenclature
    - Self-expression
- Assimilate the environmental influences, such as:
    - Alkaline (positive) influences
    - Acidic (negative) influences
    - Toxic (destructive) influences
- Assimilate psychological characteristics, such as:
    - Control (Responsibility, self-esteem, etc.)
    - Influence (Trust, Respect, Motivation, etc.)
    - Contribution (Attitude, Accountability, etc.)
    - Growth (Vision, Personal Development, etc.)
- Assimilate physiological characteristics, such as:
    - Deportment
    - Energy
    - Lifestyle

Right now you're probably feeling a bit overwhelmed! This book is not exactly what I would consider light reading. You've just concluded a full-on immersion course in changing the perception of "Who You Are" and creating the perception you desire! That's not an easy thing to accomplish and you should feel proud of yourself!

Being overwhelmed is actually a good thing because even though you feel like all that information is a big, jumbled *mess* in your head, your mind is subconsciously making all the necessary corrections to your new *Persona.* Right now, without you consciously doing anything, your mind is figuring out which additional elements you may want to incorporate in your *persona profile.* It is strategizing about your new role as the *"person who would be successful"!*

All this is happening, even though you might feel overwhelmed!

After all this information has had a chance to sink in, go back to the Modules and review the *Outline* at the beginning of each Module and see how much of the entire Module you can recall. You might surprise yourself! And if you do get stuck on a concept, you can always go back through the Module and re-read the sections you want to remember.

I would strongly suggest that you spend a week or two implementing all the techniques and strategies you learned here. When you've run through all 12 Modules, go back and do it again!

Continue to improve your new *Persona!*

WHAT'S NEXT?

What's Next?

Treat Yourself to a

V.I.P. Perception Makeover™

If you are serious about creating lasting change in your personal or professional life, I invite you to join me for a **V.I.P. Perception Makeover™**.

Together, we'll explore the endless possibilities that a **V.I.P. Perception Makeover™** has to offer!

We cut through the fog of negative self-perceptions and create new and empowering ones that will transform the way in which you live and work!

This is an intense one-day V.I.P. coaching session where you and I uncover

★ The current perceptions you have about yourself

★ How you project these perceptions onto others!

★ Why your current perceptions are now a part of your "perceived identity"!

★ Why others see you "perceived identity" as your True Identity.

★ How your "perceived identity" is sabotaging the opportunities to achieve your goals or get the results you want out of life!

If you're not

★ attracting the right partner to build an ideal relationship with

★ landing that dream job or promotion

★ feeling confident about yourself or the value you can bring to others

★ living the life you've always dreamed about . . . .

. . . it's because of the *perception* of "Who You Are"!

The **V.I.P. Perception Makeover**™ is a powerful full-day coaching session that is based on my Signature Program *"Change Your Perception, Change Yourself!"* and goes deep inside the conflict between any current perceptions you have about "WHO YOU ARE" and the new perceptions you desire!

We get right to work on identifying the perceptions that are responsible for the situation you are in today and creating the new perceptions for the person you want to become.

We will spend one full day creating new and powerful perceptions about:

☑ How you perceive other people.

☑ How other people create a perception about you,

and most importantly . . . .

☑ How you perceive yourself!

In the **V.I.P. Perception Makeover**™, you take back full control over:

★ The Perception of "Who You Are"!

★ The Perception You Desire!

★ How to project the "Perception You Desire" onto others, so that they perceive you the way in which you want to be perceived.

By applying the strategies and techniques found in my Signature Program *"Change Your Perception, Change*

Yourself!" we will create new perceptions for you and about you that are perfectly aligned with your True Identity!

I am committed to working with a limited number of highly motivated private clients who are success-driven and want to achieve permanent change in their personal or professional life.

If that describes you, please send your **V.I.P. Perception Makeover**™ scheduling request to:

coach@personacoach.com

and put **V.I.P. Perception Makeover** in the subject line.

About the Author

Allan N. Mulholland was at odds with his world for much of his life!

He became recalcitrant at an early age. He was always ready to challenge authority and found a way to do so with impunity! When he learned that he had a knack for writing, he discovered that "the pen is mightier than the sword"!

"I consider myself a man of reason. I am a liberal conservative who tries to balance social conscience with fiscal prudence. One thing our world can do without is "wingnuts", whether they be right wing or left wing! I have zero tolerance for fanatics, fakes, false prophets and fundamentalists." ~ Allan N. Mulholland

Born and raised in Holland, Allan performed poorly in high school. He was "bored"! Faced with the prospect of failing school, he convinced his parents to send him to Canada in 1965, where he completed high school and went on to get a degree in Urban Land Economics from the University of British Columbia.

At age 25, Allan began a turbulent career in Real Estate. While successful financially, he found little satisfaction in working as a realtor. He needed an outlet for his creativity and he became "bored" with selling houses.

After 6 years, Allan switched to commercial real estate and specialized in retail leasing. Soon he became a highly successful lease negotiator and an expert in contract law. He became a Director of Operations for a major real estate firm and was responsible for 10 regional shopping centers in Western Canada. But while real estate was a career, it certainly was not Allan's passion! And as he put in the long hours and late nights at the office, his first wife found comfort in the arms of another man.

They divorced in 1983.

The only thing that kept Allan "sane" throughout this difficult period was his passion for music and his talent for playing guitar. He quit his corporate job and became an entertainer on the original "Love boat", cruising the waters of the Caribbean. But after 3 months of fun and frivolity, Allan became "bored" with the lifestyle and returned to Vancouver, where he did what any self-respecting unemployed executive would do!

He printed up some business cards and became a consultant. A Retail Leasing Consultant!

With a handful of national retail chains as corporate clients, life was good for the next few years. But then disaster struck again! Allan fell in love!

With his passion for everything Italian (music, food, wine and women), Allan met a beautiful Italian *signorina* and they got married in 1987. For the next 23 years, Allan and Nadia had a volatile love/hate relationship that pitted Allan's moderate temperament against Nadia's emotional outbursts. While constantly at each other's throats, they did manage to sire three beautiful sons and to this day maintain a very strong personal bond and friendship, in spite of their divorce in 2010.

Over the past ten years, Master Results Coach & Perception Expert Allan N. Mulholland, aka "PersonaCoach", has combined his amazing insight into the human psyche with his unique ability to coach, consult and counsel. He teaches coaches how to get clients, deliver RESULTS and charge high-end coaching fees. He is the founder & president of **PersonaCoach (Int'l) LLC** and the author of *"Clients Don't Pay for Coaching. They Pay for RESULTS!"* He has helped hundreds of coaches and clients achieve RESULTS with his signature coaching program *"Change Your Perception. Change Yourself!"* The Perception of "Who You Are" is responsible for the situation you're in today, and by changing this perception you can achieve any desired outcome!

Allan is a popular keynote speaker and is often featured on radio shows, live events and tele-summits. He demonstrates in simple and straightforward language the true value and benefit of *'Change Your Perception, Change Yourself'* as it relates to relationships, career & business, wealth management, health & wellness, personal development and spiritual growth. His presentations are motivating, inspiring, thought-provoking, energizing and entertaining and he captivates his audience from start to finish.

He is also an accomplished lead guitarist and he opens many of his keynote presentations with an electrifying 'pop' rendition of Bach's Toccata that is guaranteed to get any audience 'off their seat and on their feet'!

Today Allan resides in West Vancouver, Canada and loves to go for long daily walks. He has found his "soul mate" and finally feels aligned with his world!

You can contact Allan at coach@personacoach.com

Or go to http://personacoach.com

Made in the USA
Charleston, SC
21 March 2016